Advanced Race Car Suspension Development

By Steve Smith

Editor   Steve Smith
Associate Editor   Georgiann Smith

ISBN # 0-936834-05-6

Published by

STEVE SMITH AUTOSPORTS PUBLICATIONS

P.O. Box 11631/Santa Ana, CA 92711/(714) 639-7681

TABLE OF CONTENTS

Chapter   **Page**

Taking Measurements And Making Calculations 1
Instant Center Location 3
Camber 7
Caster 16
Toe-Out 26
Bump Steer 32
Tire Slip Angle 45
The Front Beam Axle 47
Rack And Pinion Steering System 49
The Drag Strut 51
Lateral Control Linkages 53
Anti-Squat And Anti-Dive 59
Upsprung Weight 63
Wheel Rate 65
Shock Absorbers 71
The Anti Roll Bar 75
Spring Frequencies 83
Dynamic Chassis Calculations 87
Weight Distribution 95
Weight Distribution Vs Roll Couple 99
Acceleration and Deceleration Weight Transfer 105
Calculating Spring Rates 111
Banking Angle Corrections For Spring Rates 115
Structural Stiffness 121
Measuring Lateral Acceleration 139
Appendix One: Math Fundamentals 144
Appendix Two: Trig Tables 156
Appendix Three: Glossary of Terms 160
Powers And Roots Table 164
Dynamic Chassis Calculation Sheets 169

Special Thanks

A special note of thanks must go to several people who helped make this book possible. First, to Paul Lamar. Paul is a former Chaparral engineer, and a pioneer in the conception, design and development of race car wings and spoilers. He has also worked as a chassis and development consultant to Carrol Shelby racing teams, Jerry Titus racing teams, the Autocoast TI22. Can Am project, and General Motors' Pontiac division. He now owns and operates the Paul Lamar School of Race Car Design.

Other people who were a tremendous asset to us were Frank Deiny of Speedway Engineering, NASCAR driver Sonny Easley, Don Edmunds of Don Edmunds Auto Research, 1973 NASCAR Grand National champion Benny Parsons and his crew chief Travis Carter.

Taking Measurements
And Making Calculations

In many areas of this book we specify that measurements should be taken from a race car and used for calculations or for a scale drawing. These measurements should be as accurate as possible, to within a 1/16th-inch accuracy. If this tolerance is not held, the answers and conclusion you draw will be erroneous.

In making calculations, we round off decimals to two decimal points if the number is small, or to one decimal point if the total number is substantially large.

Most of these calculations are not easily made unless you have one of the new miracles of the electronic age, the electronic calculator. One which has the basic functions of add, subtract, multiply and divide will suffice. It should have a capacity for at least eight digits.

Accompanying this chapter are several drawings showing the proper way in which to take some measurements from automotive components.

The electronic calculator is the new miracle of our age, and it can prove to be a quite valuable tool for you in calculating the various items we discuss in this book. The competition among brands has brought the price of these calculators down to within the reach of everyone. If you do not already have one, it would be very helpful to you if you purchased one which included square root function.

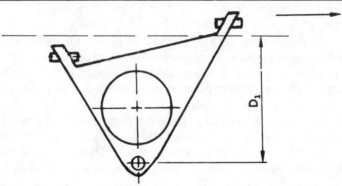

When measuring the length of an A-arm which has inner mounting points not in line with each other, the distance from the   outside mounting point to the ball joint is the length.

When measuring an upper A-arm which is curved, the straight line distance from the inner mounting point to the ball joint center is the true effective length.

Instant Center Location

The instant center is a point found by projecting lines of suspension linkage components until their intersection point is reached. The reason for doing this is to find the pivot about which the linkages rotate. The intersection point of the projected lines is the instant center, or pivot point.

The most-used instant centers are those which determine the wheel movement curve in bump and rebound and the roll center.

The other instant centers are those in the transverse plane which determine the caster change curve, anti-squat and anti-dive.

UNEQUAL LENGTH A-ARM SYSTEM

Determining the instant center of the unequal length A-arm system, whether it is employed in the front or rear suspension, is the same.

Make a scale drawing of the car's suspension layout and its positioning relative to the level ground surface. Extend a line from the center of the ball joint of the upper A-arm straight through the center of the inner pivot point of the arm and extend it a bit further into space. Draw the same type of line for the bottom A-arm, remembering to stay in the center of the ball joint straight to the center of the inner pivot point. Extend these lines into space until they intersect.

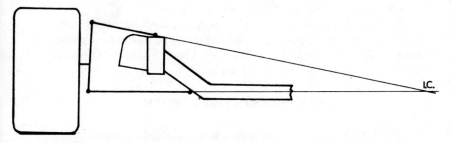

The instant center location determination of an unequal length A-arm system which converges toward the inside of the car.

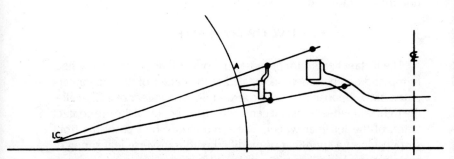

The instant center location of an unequal length A-arm system which converges toward the outside. This type of system, as shown by the arc, will always create positive camber when negative camber is required, and vice versa.

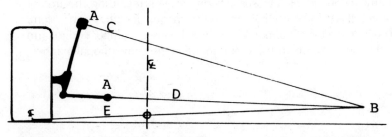

To locate the instant center for a Mac Pherson strut system, shown in the drawing as "B", line "C" is drawn at a 90-degree angle to the strut from the strut top to its intersection with the lower A-arm centerline extension ("D"). "E" shows the roll center location.

This intersection point is the instant center.

To find the roll center, a third line is drawn from the instant center to the center of the tire contact patch on the same side of the car from which the instant center line originated. Where this third line crosses the centerline of the car is the roll center.

MAC PHERSON STRUT SYSTEM

The bottom A-arm line is drawn just as described above for the unequal length A-arm system. The top line originates at the point where the strut mounts into the mounting pocket. At this point a line is drawn at a 90-degree angle to the strut downward to meet the bottom A-arm line projection.

LIVE OR BEAM AXLE

The instant center, for purposes of body roll diagrams, one-wheel bump and camber curve, is located at the center of the tire contact patch of the opposite wheel. For example, on the rear of a Chevelle, the right rear wheel's instant center lies at the center of the tire contact patch of the left rear wheel. The same would be true of the front suspension of a sprint car or modified with transverse leaf spring or cross torsion bar suspension on top of a beam axle.

CORVETTE REAR SUSPENSION

The Corvette rear suspension layout is typical of the treatment of many independent rear suspension systems regarding the instant center. It is treated just the same as the unequal length A-arm system. The half-shaft is the upper A-arm, and the lower camber control arm is the lower A-arm. Roll center is found in the conventional manner.

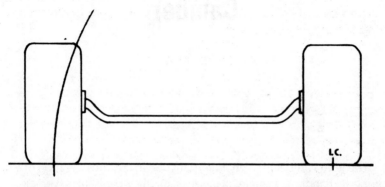

The instant center of a beam or solid axle, for purposes of one-wheel bump and camber change, is located at the center of the opposite wheel. The arc drawn here illustrates the path the wheel makes as it rotates about the instant center at the opposite wheel in one-wheel bump.

Camber

The term camber is a very important one in the consideration of a properly handling vehicle. It applies to all wheels of a vehicle, regardless of the type of suspension system employed to support the wheel.

Camber is defined as the inward or outward tilt of the wheel at the top when compared with a true vertical line at the centerline of the wheel. If a wheel had zero camber, its centerline would be a true up and down vertical line.

When the top of the wheel tilts out or away from the vehicle, the camber is positive. If the top of the wheel tilts inward toward the vehicle, the camber is negative.

The amount the wheel is tilted away from the true vertical centerline is measured in degrees.

The importance of the camber adjustment is to keep the maximum amount of tire tread on the ground during suspension movement and body roll. This positioning of the tire contact patch has a very important effect on the performance of a tire. Most racing tires will corner at their maximum with a given load and operating temperature between zero and a half a degree of negative camber. The variation depends on the particular carcass structure of the tire and the amount of deformation of the flexible tire which takes place

7

under maximum cornering conditions.

We know what the ultimate in camber is which the tire should operate at (0° to -½°), but we cannot set the camber at that and forget about it. The amount of suspension movement a chassis experiences under extreme braking and cornering means that a compromise must be reached. Because all wheels are attached to one end of a pivoting beam, the wheel's movement will not be in a true vertical line, but rather in a circular path. Knowing this, it is possible to see that the wheel is going to be moving into positive camber with any downward movement of the chassis (the object to which the pivoting beam is attached). The compromise, then, is to anticipate the amount the chassis is going to lean and then preset negative camber into the wheel. This way the wheel will still move through positive camber, but only to the point where it negates the preset negative camber, resulting in the desired zero to one-half degree negative camber.

What determines the amount which the camber is going to change during body roll? There are several factors, but before we discuss them, a few definitions are in order. First, the most common

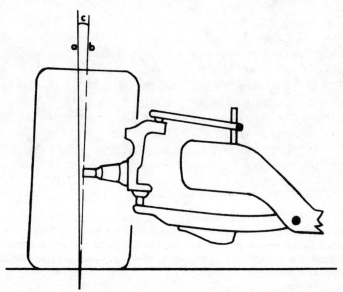

Line "A" is a true vertical line. Line "B" is the centerline of a tire set with some negative camber. "C" is the angle between "A" and "B," or the camber angle.

The cars in both of these photos are cornering at approximately the same acceleration. In fact, the one at the top is actually cornering quicker although its action
appears much less violent. The difference lies in the camber angles of the tires.
Compare the race car tire camber angles, which have been designed with proper
geometry in mind, against the passenger car camber angles, which were designed
purely for slow pleasure driving. The difference in camber angles makes a big difference in cornering speed and stability.

type of suspension linkage for an independently sprung suspension is the unequal length arms (in terms of a front suspension, the upper and lower A-arms). In our discussion of camber control, this is the type of suspension system which we will be referring to. There are other types of suspension systems which present exceptions to this system. We will discuss them separately at the end of this chapter. Another definition important to this discussion is the instant center (how to find the instant center is explained in its own chapter elsewhere in this book). The instant center is the point about which the wheel moves, describing the tire path. The instant center swing arm is the imaginary line drawn from the instant center to whatever point on the tire or suspension linkage of which you want to chart the moving path.

Four elements dictate the amount of camber change through body roll: 1) The ratio of the upper A-arm length to the lower A-arm length, 2) the static angles of the upper and lower A-arms, 3) the length of the A-arms, and 4) the spindle heighth.

In general, the longer the instant center swing arm is, the better the camber change curve is (the result is a smoother, less radical change in camber during wheel movement as compared to a shorter swing arm). Another important generalization is that the greater the ratio of length is between the upper and lower A-arms, the less linear the camber change is. This means that for every half-inch of upward wheel movement, the wheel progressively develops more negative camber. About the best ratio of upper to lower A-arm length which can be obtained for a race car built from a modified passenger car chassis is 0.6 to 1. That is, the upper A-arm has 0.6 inches of length for every 1.0 inches of length of the bottom A-arm. For a car that has a 16-inch lower A-arm, the upper A-arm would be 9.6 inches (measured from pivot point center to ball joint center). In actual practice, this ratio sometimes cannot be obtained. For example, a car with a very wide frame which is limited to a specified tread width dimension is going to have, out of necessity, shorter A-arms, especially at the top.

To chart the path of the camber change curve, first lay out a scale drawing of the front suspension of your car. To get a proper perspective of what is happening on paper, use a scale of 1"=5" (that is, one inch on paper equals five inches of measured dimension from the car).

Find the instant center and mark it on the paper. Compute the angle at which the chassis rolls (how to do this is explained elsewhere in this book). With a compass (pin point stuck in instant

ONE

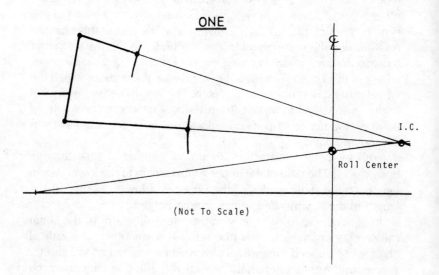

C̶L̶

I.C.

Roll Center

(Not To Scale)

TWO

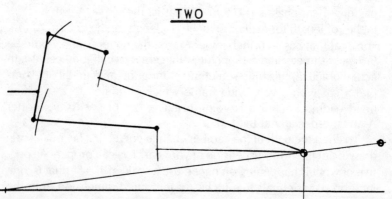

The car's body rolls about the roll center two degrees.
This dictates the arc in which the inner pivot points
move(they also move downward two degrees).

11

THREE

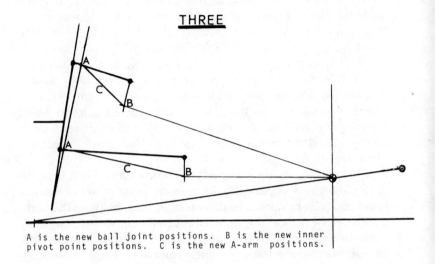

A is the new ball joint positions. B is the new inner
pivot point positions. C is the new A-arm positions.

In determining the camber change curve, the first step is to determine the instant center, then use a compass to mark the path the inner pivot points will follow as the body rolls about the roll axis. In step two, a protractor was used to determine how far the instant center line will move (if the chassis roll angle is two degrees, the new lines are drawn two degrees below the original instant center lines). From this point the compass is used to mark the arc of the movement of the ball joints. In step three, new A-arm positions are drawn. The A-arms must stay the same length and the ball joints must stay at the same height (because the height of the tire does not change), so the new A-arm positions can be drawn. Where these new A-arm ends intersect the ball joint positions drawn in step two, the new spindle upright position can be drawn between the upper and lower ball joints. The difference in angle between the static and dynamic spindle upright positions is the amount of camber change. When going through a turn with the wheels turned, the steering axis inclination will dictate more negative camber needs, of course.

center), mark the path of the inner pivot points of the A-arms (the bolts which attach the A-arms to the frame). Draw a line from the instant center to the curved path of the lower arm inner pivot at the angle which the chassis rolls (use a protractor to find this angle). Where this line intersects the curved path is the new location of the lower A-arm inner pivot when the chassis rolls. Repeat this same step for the upper A-arm. Next, use the compass to chart the movement path of the arms' ball joints (put pin end in inner pivot point of A-arms). To find the new position of the lower A-arm when the chassis rolls, draw a line the exact same length as the lower A-arm from the new position of the inner pivot point to wherever it lands on the curved movement path of the lower ball joint. Repeat this same step for the upper A-arm.

The final step in this process is to draw a vertical line from the center of the new upper ball joint position to the center of the new lower ball joint position. The difference in angle between this vertical line and a vertical line drawn through the upper and lower ball joints in their static (beginning) position is the angle of camber change (subtract the static line angle from the rolled line angle).

This amount of camber change in the suspension system is the amount of initial static camber that should be set into a car. For example, if the camber change is three degrees, then the initial camber setting should be three degrees.

However, the ultimate amount of static camber setting required may need to be changed once the car is tested on the race track. Tire size and construction and the amount of lateral acceleration the car is experiencing are three large factors that may dictate a change in the initial camber setting. The only sure method to check the amount of negative camber required by the tire once it is on the race track is to take the temperature of the tire at three places across the face of it with a tire pyrometer (the method of doing this is described in detail in *The Complete Stock Car Chassis Guide* and *The Trans Am and Corvette Chassis*. Both books are published by Steve Smith Autosports.)

OTHER SUSPENSION SYSTEMS

Although camber is a principle which affects every tire regardless of the suspension system attached to it, not every suspension system is adjustable for camber.

In the live or beam axle, the instant center for body roll and one-wheel bump is the center of the tire contact patch of the opposite wheel. For example, to find the path of the camber change of the right rear wheel of a Chevelle, put the pin point of a compass at the center of the tire contact patch of the left rear wheel, and draw the line from the center of the contact patch of the right rear wheel.

The solid axle is not adjustable for any camber, though. If it is found—by use of a tire pyrometer—that the tire is experiencing excessive positive or negative camber, the axle (in terms of a solid front beam axle) or housing (in terms of a solid rear axle) can be carefully bent to compensate for the difference.

In actual practice, bending the rear end housing of a car to gain one-half to one degree of negative camber is not worth the trouble it requires. Of cars we know of which have tried this, the maximum gain in lateral acceleration has been 0.05 G. The rear wheels are not nearly as subject to radical camber changes as are the front wheels because the roll couple distribution is always heavily biased toward the front end of the vehicle.

On a car with a solid beam front axle, however, a careful check of the camber should be made with a pyrometer. If persistent problems of excessive positive or negative camber appear, the axle should be bent to compensate for it.

Cars equipped with the Mac Pherson strut suspension system are not generally adjustable for camber. However, a slight modification can be made to make it fully adjustable. This should be done on any Mac Pherson system car which is used in competition.

The Datsun 240-Z uses the Mac Pherson strut-type suspension at the rear as well as the front. Here is illustrated a Mac Tilton-built Datsun with the sliding aluminum plate which makes the strut adjustable for camber.

The best system we have seen was designed by Mac Tilton and used on the BRE and Tilton-built competition Datsuns. A hole is cut in the strut-retaining portion of the top of the sheet-metal tower. Then a slotted aluminum plate is bolted into the hole. Another aluminum plate is bolted to the top of the strut. This plate has threaded extensions which protrude into the slots of the strut retaining plate. This allows the strut to be moved laterally to adjust camber.

Caster

Caster is a major factor which provides a vehicle with directional stability. Directional stability is the ability of the vehicle to travel straight ahead with a minimum of steering corrections by the driver.

Caster is interrelated with another stability factor, steering axis inclination, but this will be discussed later.

Viewing a suspension system from the side, positive caster is defined as the backward tilt of the steering axis (backward toward the rear of the vehicle), and negative caster is the forward tilt of the steering axis. Caster is measured in the degrees of angle the steering axis lies from a true vertical line.

The steering axis line is the vertical line drawn from the upper to the lower ball joints on a double A-arm independent syspension system. On a solid beam front axle, the steering axis is the angle of the kingpins in the side view, and is adjusted for caster by lengthening or shortening the strut rods which attach the axle to the vehicle.

To understand the principle and effect of caster in the steering system, it is easiest to examine the ordinary household furniture caster.

When a piece of furniture on casters is pushed, the casters turn in their pivots until the wheels are in line with the direction of force applied and the wheels are trailing in back of the pivot. In this

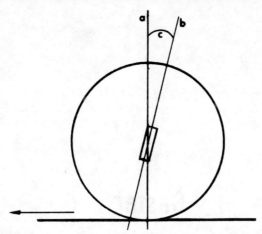

This illustrates a positive caster angle. The arrow points in the direction of the front of the vehicle. "A" is the true vertical line. "B" is the centerline of the spindle upright, which is tilted back. "C" is the difference in angle between "A" and "B," which is the positive caster angle.

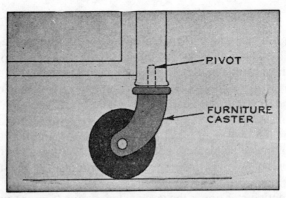

The ordinary furniture caster demonstrates why the wheel centerline must trail behind the pivot point.

position, the furniture will roll easily and in a straight line.

Therefore, it can be seen that when a force is applied to the pivot it tends to drag the wheel behind it. The reason lies in the fact that the projected centerline of the caster pivot strikes the floor in front of the contact patch of the wheel.

This same principle applies to a vehicle. If the steering axis pivot is tilted backward at the top, the projected centerline of the pivot strikes the ground ahead of the tire contact patch (which is positive caster). When the vehicle is driven forward, the pivot drags the wheel behind it giving the car directional stability.

There is a moment arm which exists between the projected line of the pivot and the tire contact patch. This moment arm exerts a torque around the steering axis. With the wheel aligned in positive caster, this torque acts to force the wheel in a straight ahead direction. When a wheel is aligned with negative caster, this same torque works to accentuate any steering input into the wheel.

As the caster angle is increased in the positive direction, the effort required to steer the car away from its straight ahead course and hold it in a turn will be increased. The tendency of the car to straighten out more rapidly when leaving a turn for the straightway is also increased by increasing positive caster.

HOW MUCH CASTER?

For the competition vehicle the amount of caster set into a chassis depends on two factors: the weight of the vehicle and the amount of weight on the front wheels, and the feel of the steering to the driver.

For race cars that weigh 3,500 pounds and more, front caster angles usually run between three and five degrees positive. The intermediate of four degrees is usually the maximum for most drivers in view of the steering effort they can endure over the course of a race.

For vehicles that weigh in the neighborhood of 2,000 to 2,600 pounds, six degrees of positive camber are generally employed.

CASTER STAGGER

At any track where the car is making only left turns, the caster is staggered with more positive caster in the right front than in the left front. The reason for using caster stagger is to help the wheels steer themselves to the left into the corners.

For short track racing, many drivers prefer to use as much caster stagger as possible (up to a maximum, usually, of about four degrees). The greater amount of stagger will allow the driver to almost relax the steering wheel completely entering a turn, letting the car steer itself into the corner.

The drawback of using so much caster stagger, though, is the increased effort in crossing the steering wheel over to the right to

18

correct for oversteer. The greater the stagger, the greater the effort required to turn the wheel back past the straight ahead centerline of the steering wheel.

The higher the speed of the race track, the more the caster stagger closes up. At Daytona International Speedway, for example, drivers generally use no more than 1½ degrees of caster stagger.

The amount of caster stagger is totally up to the driver's preference, and several settings should be tried before the final setting is arrived at.

MEASURING THE CASTER ANGLE

To measure caster, a caster gauge and wheel degree plates are necessary. Start with the right front wheel. Turn it 20 degrees to the left (as measured on the wheel degree plate). Zero the caster gauge. Turn the wheel back to straightahead then to 20 degrees to the right and read the caster angle in degrees on the gauge. Repeat these same steps for the left front wheel.

After setting the caster, it will be noted that (with most types of suspension systems) a change in caster also creates a change in camber and toe. A certain amount of chasing back and forth in setting the front end is inevitable. But one thing which will help save much time is to make note of what effect one turn of an adjustment has on camber, caster and toe.

CASTER PATTERN

In a separate section elsewhere in this book, anti-dive is fully explained. But it is important to mention it here because the anti-dive angles have a direct bearing on the car's caster setting. If any amount of anti-dive at all is contained in the front suspension system, a change in the caster angle is created when the suspension moves into bump or rebound. The only way to insure no change of the caster angle is to have the upper and lower A-arms, in the side view plane, running parallel to each other and parallel to the ground.

Many leading racing teams in all types of racing—stock cars, Indy cars, Can Am cars, Trans Am cars, etc.—have tried employing a certain amount of anti-dive in the front suspension. But the results of the experiment have always been that it is far better to have no anti-dive whatsoever and experience no change in caster. Caster change can be a very unstable situation, making the car's steering

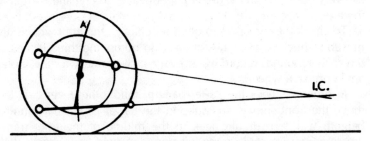

The arc marked "A" is the path of caster change caused by an anti-dive angle placement of the A-arm mounting points. Caster change should be minimized to zero, if possible.

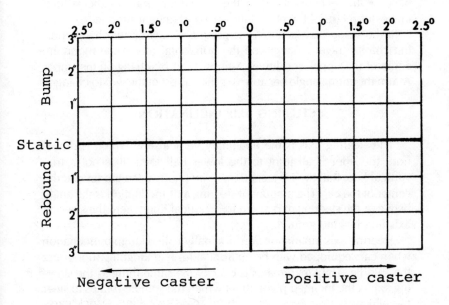

This is the type of chart which should be used for determining the amount of caster change present in your suspension system.

feel very "twitchy" to the driver under heavy braking and cornering forces.

To check the car's pattern of caster change, the front wheels are moved through three inches of travel in bump and three inches of travel in rebound, recording at every inch of the way the caster angle on each wheel.

In order to check the caster pattern, follow these steps: 1) Remove the front springs and support the car at its normal running heighth with a hydraulic jack in the middle of the front frame crossmember. 2) Replace the left front and right front shocks with dummy shocks (old worn shocks that have been drilled and the fluid drained so they offer no resistance). 3) Let the running heighth of the car down one inch with the hydraulic jack. Take caster angle reading of both front wheels and record the angle on your chart. 4) Continue this same step letting the car's running heighth down in one-inch increments to a total of three inches to simulate three full inches of bump travel of the wheels. 5) Return the car to the starting height with the hydraulic jack, then move it upward to check three inches of rebound travel and the caster change it produces.

If the suspension geometry is producing any caster change during chassis travel, change (on the horizontal plane) the mounting angle of the upper and lower A-arms. Start by changing the upper A-arm mounting angle because it is the easiest of the two to change.

STEERING AXIS INCLINATION

The steering axis is the imaginary vertical line which is drawn from the upper ball joint to the lower ball joint. It is not a true vertical line. Rather, it is leaned in, or inclined, at the top toward the center of the car. The amount of steering axis inclination is the angle between the steering axis and a true vertical line where the steering axis line hits the ground.

Steering axis inclination was originally called kingpin inclination when cars equipped with beam front axles had kingpins supporting the spindle. The kingpin axis is exactly the same thing as the steering axis—the inclined pivot about which the spindle rotates to steer the wheel.

The reasons for having steering axis inclination are threefold: 1) directional stability, 2) to distribute the weight of the vehicle evenly on the entire spindle arm support, and 3) to add negative camber to the wheel during suspension bounce position so an excessive amount of static negative camber need not be added to the car.

21

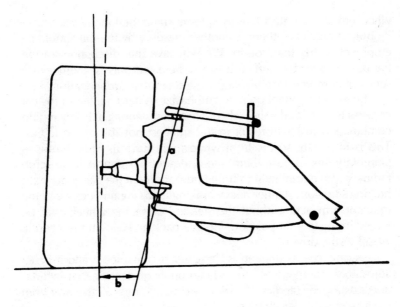

"A" is the steering axis inclination line. "B" is the scrub radius.

SCRUB RADIUS

An important term that comes into play with steering axis inclination is scrub radius. To picture what the scrub radius is, imagine the steering axis line projected all the way down to the ground. Now picture the centerline of the tire contact patch. The distance which exists between the steering axis line and the tire centerline at the ground is the scrub radius.

The length of the scrub radius varies greatly depending on three things: the tread width of the tire, the amount of outside wheel offset and the angle of the steering axis inclination.

When the wheel is steered, the tire actually rotates on this scrub radius.

During forward travel of the wheels, a force applied through the centerline of the tire creates a torque on the scrub radius. The scrub radius distance becomes a moment arm acting about the steering axis, with the net effect being a tendency for the front wheels to toe-out during straightahead travel. This is the one single reason why static toe-in is set into the front suspension of passenger cars. The longer the scrub radius distance is, the more tendency for the wheels to toe-out, thus requiring more static toe-in.

But on race cars, there is another reason why toe-out should be employed rather than toe-in. We will save that discussion for the toe-out chapter, but suffice it to say here that this is another in a series of compromises required in setting a car up perfectly.

The most important point to emphasize in this chapter for the car constructor is to find a tire, wheel offset and steering axis inclination combination that will result in the smallest possible scrub radius. This is important so the front wheels will have as little torque as possible trying to push them into a toe-out position. A large scrub radius is also detrimental to front end stability of the car under hard braking situations. Under heavy braking loads (again because of the moment arm acting about the steering axis), the wheels will be forced into a toe-out position, feeding back a "kick" in the steering wheel to the driver.

Steering axis inclination is designed into a spindle and it is not adjustable. There are all possible amounts of steering axis inclination existing in spindles of various manufacturers, all the way from three degrees to ten degrees.

It has been found with most stock cars that a spindle containing from 5 to 7½ degrees of steering axis inclination works best. If it is possible to use the spindle (considering its other aspects such as steering arm design and spindle upright heighth), the one with 7½ degrees would be more desirable.

It is important to note that when constructing a car, the amount of steering axis inclination of the right front spindle must be exactly the same as the inclination of the left front spindle. If the inclination were not exactly the same, the torque feedback around the pivot caused by the length of the scrub radius would not be equal left and right. The result would be a hard pull to one side under hard braking conditions.

One cannot assume that just because he has purchased two spindles from the same manufacturer they have the exact same inclination angle. We have found, through measuring spindles, the inclination angles contained in one spindle model of a popular manufacturer vary as much as three degrees. The only way to be sure is to measure the spindle with an inclinometer.

REVOLVING THE SPINDLE

Turning the wheels, as in making a turn to the left or right, revolves the spindle around the steering axis pivot. Because the

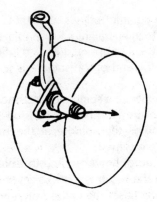

The spindle follows an upside down "u" path as it is rotated about the steering axis.

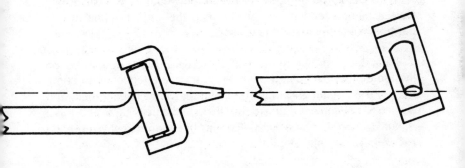

pivot axis is inclined, the path the spindle follows as it turns the wheel will be a curved path rather than a straight path. In exaggerated form, the path the spindle follows is an upside down "u." So, if the pivot stays in a fixed position, the end of the spindle is lower after it has been turned.

However, when the wheel is in place, the spindle end cannot be lowered because the heighth of the tire is a fixed dimension that cannot be changed. The wheel holds the spindle at the same heighth no matter how the wheels are turned.

The spindle end is still trying to drop, however, and this places an upward force against the pivot. The result is that the pivot (the spindle upright) is raised. This in turn raises the entire front end of the vehicle (to a small degree).

With gravity pulling downward on the weight of the car, it will have a natural tendency to try to keep the weight at the lowest position possible toward the ground.

It can be seen with the weight of the car pushing downward on the force-raised spindle, the wheels will have a tendency to come back to the straight ahead position after they have been turned, and also resist any force tending to turn them in the first place. This force is not enough to cause hard steering, but is sufficient to provide excellent directional stability.

A SIDE EFFECT

A side effect of steering axis inclination is the fact that this upside down "u" path the spindle follows causes the wheel to go into positive camber. The greater the angle of steering axis inclination, the greater the force toward positive camber as the wheels are turned.

The way to offset some of this positive camber inherent in the situation is by using positive caster. The higher the inclination angle, the higher the amount of positive caster required to offset it.

On a stock car equipped with a spindle having 5 to 7½ degrees of steering axis inclination, 4 degrees of positive caster is sufficient to offset the positive camber problem.

Toe-Out

Toe-in or toe-out is the difference in distance, measured in fractions of an inch, between the extreme front and the extreme rear of the tires at spindle heighth.

We have already discussed in the steering axis inclination chapter why passenger cars need a static alignment of toe-in. While all passenger cars are set with static toe-in for stability in straight ahead driving, race cars are set with static toe-out because the front wheel geometry must be correct for the turns and not necessarily the straightaways, hence a compromise.

ACKERMAN STEERING VERSUS TOE-IN

The modern race car suspension, no matter what type of vehicle, should not have any amount of Ackerman built into the steering geometry. The Ackerman theory is the design principle which states that for any given corner the outside wheel should have less steering lock because it is running at a larger radius than the inside wheel. Ackerman is designed into the suspension by angling both the left front and right front steering arms inward toward the centerline of the vehicle from the lower ball joints, with the projected lines converging at the centerline of the rear end housing.

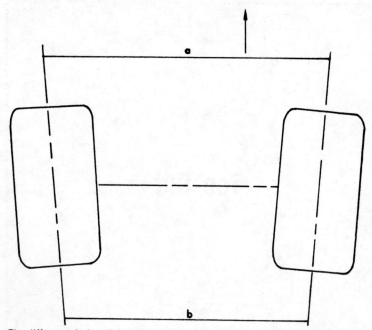

The difference in length between "A" and "B" is the amount of toe-out. The arrow indicates the direction of travel of the car.

This will not work in a race car for two reasons: 1) If the steering arms were angled inward from the lower ball joint, bump steer would result in most cases (for clarification of this, see the bump steer chapter elsewhere in this book). 2) Owing to weight transfer, the outside wheel always runs at a higher loading than the inside wheel, and therefore at a greater slip angle which necessitates greater steering lock.

If the Ackerman principle were to be applied to a racing car, the inside wheel would be forced to toe-out past its proper turning radius and thus create more tire drag, in turn slowing the cornering speed of the vehicle. This steering theory as used in a race car is called the Anti-Ackerman principle.

THE NEED FOR TOE-OUT

What is proper for a race car is straight steering arms with the tie rod end centerline being straight in line with the lower ball joint centerline. With equal length tie rods on the left and right sides, this means the inside wheel will be turned the same amount as the

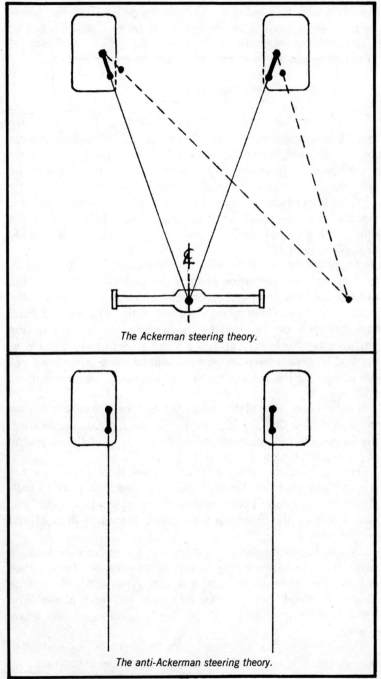

The Ackerman steering theory.

The anti-Ackerman steering theory.

28

outside wheel, thus trying to force the inside wheel to toe-in in a turn. A slight amount of static toe-out (from 1/32-inch out to 3/16-inch out, depending on the size of the radius) is set into the front end to put the inside wheel on its proper radius.

SETTING THE TOE-OUT

Because the toe setting is defined as the total difference in distance between the two tires at a specific point, most people assume they can properly set the toe using both wheels. This is incorrect for a very precise alignment, which is what is required for a racing vehicle.

If the total overall toe-out of a pair of wheels is measured, it is possible that toe-in will result on one wheel and toe-out on the other, with the total alignment still being correct. This is a highly unstable condition.

To set the toe-out of the wheels individually, it is first necessary to determine the centerline of the car's suspension. Measure the distance between the inner pivot point of the lower A-arms of the front suspension. Determine the center of the distance and mark that centerline on the front frame crossmember. Paint it on the crossmember, or better yet, run a small straight bead of weld to mark it. This is a reference point you will be using many times, not just to reset the toe-out, but to make other chassis measurements as well.

Find the centerline of the chassis at the rear of the vehicle following a procedure similar to the one for the front, measuring between the frame rails, or suspension mounting points. Mark the centerline of the rear on the chassis as well.

Having found the centerline of the chassis, mark it visually either with a string stretched between two jack stands or with a small-dimension aluminum I-beam resting on top of two jack stands. For easy reference this bisecting line should extend in front of and behind the car.

Before beginning the toe setting, make sure both tie rods are equal in length. When setting the toe, be sure to shorten or lengthen both tie rods an equal amount. If the rods are not the exact same length, the steering box will be off center and more play will be introduced into the steering wheel due to lash in the steering box gears.

A second reference line must be constructed outside the wheel to be aligned. This again can be an aluminum I-beam supported by jack stands. Measure at both ends of this beam number two to the chassis centerline. The distance at both ends of number two beam must be exactly the same so it is determined that the number two beam is exactly parallel to the car's centerline. Making accurate measurements here is absolutely critical! A difference of 1/32-inch can make a big difference in toe setting. Make sure, too, that the number two beam is satisfactorily secured to the base holding it at each end so it cannot be accidentaly knocked out of alignment during toe setting operations.

To set the toe, use a very exacting measurement device such as a vernier caliper or machinists' rule. Measure from the beam number two to a flat portion on the outer edge of the metal wheel at both the front and the rear of the wheel. If the front measurement is "a" inches and the rear measurement is "b" inches, then "a minus b" is the toe-out.

To determine the toe-out per wheel, divide the total amount of toe-out needed by two.

AN EXAMPLE

Let's say we need a total toe-out of ⅛-inch. The toe-out per wheel would be ⅛ divided by 2, or 1/16-inch per wheel.

We are starting at the right front wheel on a car whose tie rods are behind the spindles. If the measurement at the front of the wheel is ¼-inch from the beam number two to the wheel, and the measurement from the rear of the wheel to the beam is ¼-inch, then ¼–¼ equals zero, meaning there is no toe-out. To set 1/16-inch toe-out into the wheel, the tie rod has to be shortened until the "front minus rear" measurements equal 1/16-inch.

Repeat these same steps for the left front wheel.

TOE AT THE REAR

So far, we have been concerned primarily with the toe settings in the front wheels. But many cars with independent rear suspension are adjustable also for toe at the rear.

Hard acceleration and deceleration loads force the tires into a toe-out position. Because the rear wheels are not performing a steering function, thus causes tire scrub and thus is undesirable. So, toe-in is used at the rear.

Depending on the amount of acceleration the engine delivers to the rear wheels, anywhere from 1/32 to 1/8-inch per wheel is used. The greatest amount of toe-in would be applicable to a highly powered car such as a Can Am or Indy car. A Corvette would use about 1/16-inch per wheel at the most. Lightly powered cars such as a Formula Vee or Formula Ford would require the 1/32-inch per wheel.

Bump Steer

Bump steer is a common front suspension geometry problem which results from the steering tie rod moving in a path which is dissimilar to the path in which the wheel it is connected to is moving.

Bump steer can also be present in the rear suspension caused by improper linkage of suspension components, but this area will be treated separately.

Visualize the path a front wheel makes as it moves straight up and down. Its path is a curved one (called an arc). This path is curved because the A-arm which attaches it to the chasis is securely fastened and is only free to move in a circle around the bolt securing it. An arc, when speaking in terms of geometry, is treated the same as a circle. From the center of the circle to the outside circumference of it is the radius. In the front end of a car, the instant center swing arm is the radius of the tire path. The circumference of the circle or arc is the path the tire follows at its centerline.

The tie rod also moves in a similar type of arc. The center of its circle is the centerline of the inner tie rod end where it attaches to the steering cross link. The length of the tie rod is the radius of it. The circumference of the arc or circle of the tie rod is the path the centerline of the outer tie rod end follows as it moves.

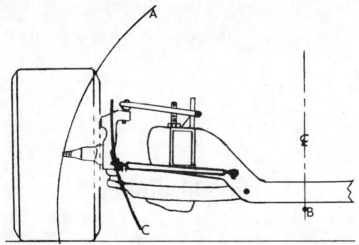

A typical bump steer problem is illustrated here (in exaggerated form for clarity). "A" is the path of the wheel about the instant center. "C" is the path of the tie rod end attached to the steering arm. If the steering arm is located behind the spindle, this dissimilarity in arcs will cause a toe-in problem in bump. If the steering arm is in front of the spindle, the wheel will toe-out in bump.

In order to have a wheel which moves in bump and rebound while remaining pointed straight ahead (which is the definition of no bump steer), then the arc of the outer tie rod end and the arc of the wheel path must have the same circle center. If the inner tie rod end is situated in a position that is *not* at the center of the arc described by the wheel, then the wheel will be forced to steer in or out as it travels to its vertical limits.

For zero bump steer, the tie rod ("d" in the accompanying drawing) must intersect the instant center and its length must be within the confines of planes A and B.

The tie rod can be moved outside planes A and B, but its length (d) must still remain the same as the position as if it were inside the planes, and it still must intersect the instant center.

The easiest way to build the steering geometry for a stock car is to locate the centerline of the outer tie rod end directly in line with the centerline of the lower ball joint, and the inner tie rod end centerline directly in line with the centerline of the lower A-arm attachment bolt.

Because positive caster has a direct effect on bump steer, the tie rod, viewed in the top view plane, must be running parallel to the centerline projection of the spindle *after* the intended static caster setting is made.

33

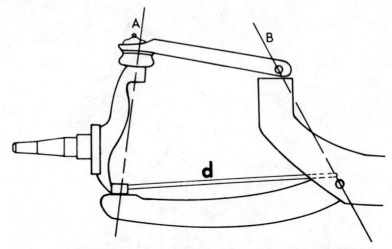

The tie rod must fall between the confines of planes "A" and "B," and the tie rod's centerline must intersect the instant center. The tie rod may be laterally displaced so long as the length remains the same as if it were between "A" and "B," and the centerline still intersects the instant center. This will yield zero bump steer.

MEASURING THE BUMP STEER

There are any number of ways to measure bump steer. The most accurate way, however, is one which treats each front wheel separately.

To measure the bump steer, first clamp the steering wheel tight where the wheels are in the straight ahead position. Next, remove the springs and shock absorbers and place the car on blocks at the center of the front crossmember which places it at its normal ride heighth.

On the wheel you intend to start with, remove the wheel and tire assembly and replace with a wheel minus the tire. Clamp a plate on the wheel with vise grips. The plate is marked in one-inch increments to measure bounce and rebound movements of the wheel. Position a stand on which two dial indicators are mounted next to the plate (with the indicator needles compressed half their travel distance).

Place a hydraulic jack under the lower A-arm and begin moving it up in one-inch increments. Move it through three inches of rebound and three inches of bump travel. At each one-inch increment take a toe reading. Read the number on the dial indicator at the front of the wheel and the number at the rear of the wheel. The difference

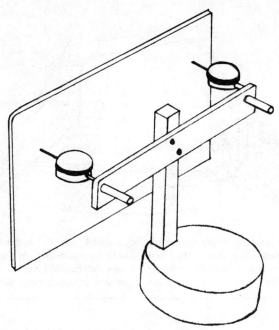

The bump steer checking equipment described in the text. The plate at the back is the one which is clamped to the wheel.

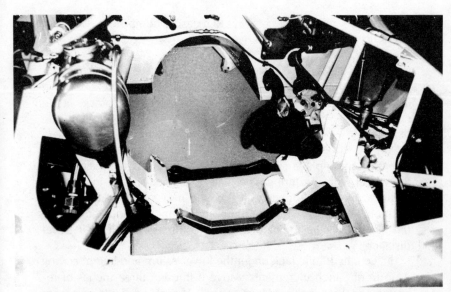

This is the engine bay of the 1974 Penske Matador. Notice the custom-built steering cross shaft which mounts the tie rod ends directly in line with the lower A-arm pivot point. The tie rod centerlne lies exactly parallel to the lower A-arm centerline, so the tie rod intersects the instant center.

35

This is another method of building a custom steering cross shaft. The problem here was that engine clearance problems would not let the cross shaft set any higher, so ears for the tie rod mounts were flame-cut and welded onto the cross shaft at the required point. The cross shaft was made out of 1"×2" bar stock.

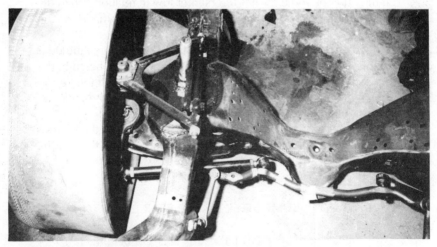

This is a tie rod mounted with a stock Chevy steering cross shaft. Notice that the outer tie rod end is in direct line with the ball joint. Being the tie rod extends inward past the lower A-arm inner pivot point, the tie rod is longer than the confines of planes "A" and "B." There will be a bump steer problem here.

36

in the two numbers is the toe measurement. If the rear number is larger, the wheel has toe-in. If the front number is larger, the wheel has toe-out.

A typical bump steer pattern for a well designed race car will allow no more than 0.015-inch of toe-in or toe-out through three full inches of bump travel.

Be sure before beginning bump steer measurement, the front end alignment has been set to the desired application specifications. If tie rod changes are necessary to correct for any bump steer, be sure to reset the front end alignment.

MAKING BUMP STEER CORRECTIONS

For the steering system which utilizes the steering box, pitman arm, idler arm and steering cross shaft, the correction can be made by installing a custom-made steering cross shaft.

The shaft will mount to the pitman arm and idler arm in the conventional manner, but its attachment points for the inner tie rod ends will be moved to the point determined necessary. This may also necessitate new shorter or longer tie rods.

If the outer tie rod ends lies too high or low in relationship to the lower ball joint, a new steering arm can be custom-made for the spindle.

With the rack and pinion steering system, a little more latitude is available. If the inner tie rod ends are not at the correct heighth, the entire rack can be repositioned up or down to correct. If the tie rod is running at an angle due to a positive caster setting, the rack can be repositioned forward or rearward to correct the angle.

If spherical rod end bearings are used at the ends of the tie rods instead of the traditional tapered automotive tie rod end, the bearing can be shimmed if its heighth is not correct.

BUMP STEER AT THE REAR

The angles and heights of the linkages connecting the rear wheels to the chassis dictate the amount and type of bump steer the rear wheels encounter as the body rolls.

If the outside rear wheel is forced to toe out during body roll, the car will experience roll oversteer. If the outside rear wheel is forced to toe-in during body roll, the car will experience roll understeer. Roll understeer is the more stable of the two characteristics, although both should be eliminated to as great a degree as is possible.

Note: The perfect bump steer graph showing absolute lack of bump steer would have the plotted line running straight up and down on top of the 0 line.

BUMP STEER PROBLEM CURVES FOR TIE RODS MOUNTED BEHIND THE SPINDLE

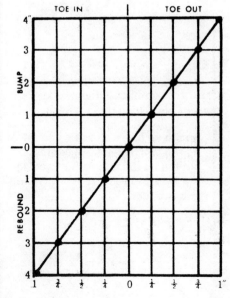

The sloped line at left indicates the outer tie rod end is too high or the inner tie rod end is too low. To correct, shim the outer tie rod end to lower it.

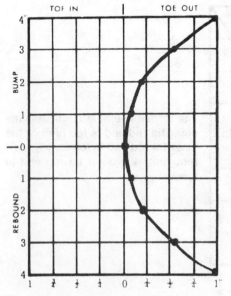

At right, the wheel is toeing-in on bump and out in rebound. The cause is the outer tie rod end is too low or inner is too high.

A convex curve like this indicates tie rod end heights are compatible but the tie rod is too short causing the wheel to toe out in both bump and rebound.

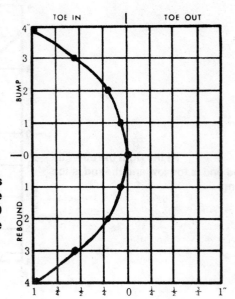

The curve at the right is the same basic problem as the one on the bottom of page 39 except the tie rod is too long here causing toe-in.

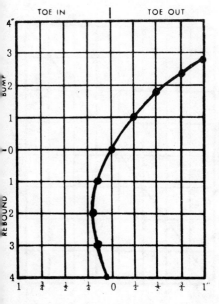

Here are two examples of combination problems. At left the outer tie rod end is too high and the tie rod is too short.

At the right the outer tie rod end is too low and the rod is too long.

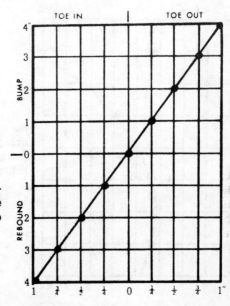

BUMP STEER PROBLEM CURVES FOR TIE RODS MOUNTED IN FRONT OF THE SPINDLE

At right, the wheel is toeing-in on bump and out in rebound. The cause is the outer tie rod end is too low or inner is too high.

41

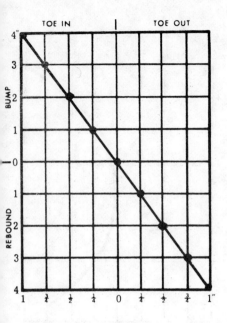

The sloped line at left indicates the outer tie rod end is too high or the inner tie rod end is too low. To correct, shim the outer tie rod end to lower it.

A convex curve like this indicates tie rod end heights are compatible but the tie rod is too short causing the wheel to toe-in in both bump and rebound.

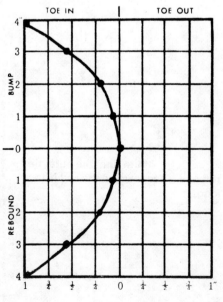

The tie rod is too long here causing toe-out.

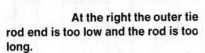

At the right the outer tie rod end is too low and the rod is too long.

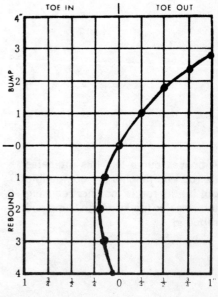

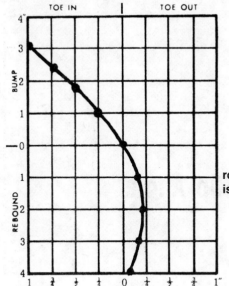

At left the outer tie rod end is too high and the tie rod is too short.

Tire Slip Angle

A tire's slip angle is defined as the difference between the aimed direction of the tire (as it passes through the tire contact patch centerline) and the actual direction of tire travel (where the tire is actually headed).

Why doesn't a car travel in the path its front wheels point? Because the tire contact patch is flexing against the tire carcass, which is caused by lateral acceleration forces. This makes the actual tire footprint offset at an angle from the true tire centerline. The difference in this deviation is the slip angle.

Most high performance racing tires are designed to operate with a maximum of five degrees of slip angle. If the tire is overloaded beyond this slip angle, its performance (meaning traction ability) drops off tremendously. Increased weight transfer onto an outside tire during a turn increases the slip angle the tire is running at. This is why tire size must increase as weight and weight transfer do. (The increased slip angle of the tire with more weight is due to the fact that the coefficient of friction of a tire decreases with increasing load.)

There are many interrelating factors affecting tire performance, including operating temperature, inflation pressure, lateral acceleration, downforce load and camber angle. For complete information about these effects on tire performance, read the chapter "Racing Tires" in *The Complete Stock Car Chassis Guide* or *The Trans Am and Corvette Chassis,* both published by Steve Smith Autosports.

DETERMINING THE ANGLE OF SLIP

The angle of slip the rear tires are generating in any corner can be determined graphically after first taking some data.

The data required is measuring at what angle the front wheels are turned in a corner. This may be taken by a mechanical device which is connected by chain and roller to the steering wheel. At the other end, another roller has a marking device attached to it which makes a line on a rolling strip of paper. This will record the angle at which the steering wheel is turned. From this information, the amount at which the front wheels are turned can be obtained. To do this, divide the angle at which the steering wheel is turned by the overall steering ratio. For example, the overall steering ratio is 20 to 1 and the steering wheel is turned 47 degrees. How much are the front wheels turned? Divide 47 by 20, which equals 2.35 degrees. The overall steering ratio is obtained by placing the front wheels of the vehicle on wheel degree plates. An inclinometer is placed at the center of the steering wheel when the wheels are in the straight ahead position. The steering wheel is turned until the degree plates read one degree. The angle shown on the inclinometer is the ratio of steering wheel angle per degree of wheel angle.

Once this data is obtained, lay out a scale drawing of the car and its four wheels on paper. Draw the front wheels turned in the angle which they are turned during the corner in question. Project the centerlines of the left and right spindles to the inside of the turn until they intersect. This intersection is the center of rotation of the car through the turn. From the center of rotation, draw lines to the centerline of the tire contact patch of the left rear and right rear tires. At this intersection point, draw a line at a 90-degree angle to the line from the center of rotation. The angle between the line and the tire centerline is the slip angle of the rear tires. A large slip angle will indicate oversteer. A small angle will indicate understeer. If the car is balanced the outside tire slip angles should not exceed 5 degrees.

46

The Front Beam Axle

For years many race car constructors have used the solid beam front axle with the argument that it affords greater strength.

Sticking to this argument is very costly in terms of the better handling qualities their cars could experience if equipped with independent front suspension.

The drawbacks to the solid beam front axle are many. Among them: 1) There is a gyroscopic coupling force under bump causing axle tramp (an oscillation between front wheels which destroys steering linkage strength), 2) It has a high amount of unsprung weight, 3) It has a very high roll center.

The strength of an independent front suspension is not a problem. The only thing required for the chassis to absorb the loads placed on it in a different position when independent suspension is added is to be sure all the mounting points are well-triangulated. How this is carried out is discussed in the "Structural Stiffness" chapter elsewhere in this book.

This independent suspension midget was constructed by Don Edmunds. It has been driven against conventional midgets on all types of tracks and has proven in every case it is superior.

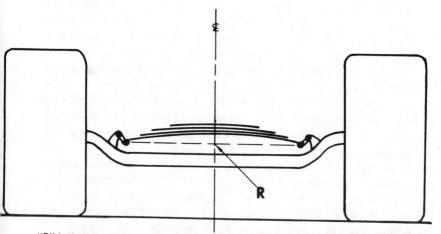

"R" is the roll center location of this beam axle with transverse leaf spring. Because the spring is anchored to the chassis, only half of the spring's weight contributes to unsprung weight.

Rack And Pinion Steering System

RACK AND PINION STEERING SYSTEM

The rack and pinion steering system is the most direct and accurate type of steering gear. It is small, light, compact, sensitive and easy to mount. It affords an effective feedback from the wheels to the steering wheel, and it is very easy to minutely change its mounting positioning to help adjust a bump steer problem.

Most rack and pinion steering systems are composed of a steel tube in which the steering rack slides. The rack is a rod with gear teeth cut along it (either spur or helical gears). A pinion at the end of the steering column meshes with the rack to cause it to move back and forth. On each end of the rack are connected the tie rods which pull or push the steering arms of the spindles.

Because of the light weight and construction of this type of steering unit, it is not practical to use on a competition car weighing any more than 2,800 pounds. It is ideally suited, however, to the NASCAR-type modifieds, sprint cars, super modifieds, midgets, and other classes of cars in these weight categories.

The easiest place to obtain one of these rack and pinion units is from a passenger car already equipped with one. The Ford Pinto, the Datsun 240-Z and the Jaguar XKE are three cars which employ the rack and pinion system. Of the three, the Jaguar system is the beefiest. It also has an advantage in that it bolts to its crossmember mount in the chassis, rather than being "C-clamped" as are the other two. A problem found with the Pinto rack is that it flexes excessively when used with wide racing tread tires or any racing type of offset wheel.

A rack and pinion steering system fitted on a NASCAR modified.

The Drag Strut

THE DRAG STRUT

Stock cars such as the later model Ford, or those with the Grand National front racing snout section, have lower A-arms which have only one inner attachment point, rather than two attachment points such as the Chevelle lower A-arm.

To stabilize this lower control arm from fore and aft compliance, a drag strut (also known as a tension rod or compression rod in cars such as the Datsuns) braces it against the chassis.

In most stock applications of a drag strut, it is anchored to the chassis in a semihard rubber bushing. For racing purposes, this rubber bushing, no matter how hard it is, must be replaced with a steel monoball component.

To explain why this change must be made, picture a car under heavy braking loads. The lower control arm is forcing the drag strut rearward with extreme tension loads. The drag strut, in turn, is braced against the chassis by this rubber bushing. If the rubber bushing compresses the least bit, a change in caster and toe will result, giving an instability in driver feel and lessened stopping power.

The replacement kit is pictured here. It is available from Steve Smith Autosports.

51

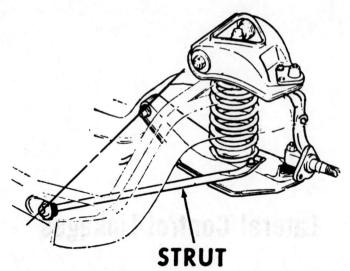

STRUT

The drag strut forms the second side of the lower A-arm. The lower arm and strut function together as one unit just as if they were one solid A-arm.

The stock-type rubber bushing on the drag strut, at top right, is replaced by the steel monoball unit, below, which allows the strut vertical movement but no forward movement.

The steel monoball unit is mounted into this steel adaptor bracket which is welded into the hole in the chassis occupied by the rubber bushing.

Lateral Control Linkages

Solid beam axles (both at the front and rear of a vehicle) need a lateral locating device attaching them to the chassis. This is done so the body will not shift sideways on the axle, placing a shear stress situation on the suspension linkage points and springs.

The most common forms of control linkages being used are the Watts linkage, the Panhard bar and the Jacob's ladder.

WATT'S LINKAGE

The ideal car has zero roll steer and bump steer which prevents it from feeling "twitchy" in turns and over bumps. A Watts linkage is the only type of lateral control linkage which results in zero roll steer.

The Watts linkage has a bellcrank which is attached to the center of the rear end housing on a pivot. It has two arms from the bellcrank, one extending in each direction, ultimately anchoring in a bracket on each side of the chassis. Each end of both these arms are free to pivot in spherical rod end bearings.

This system keeps the chassis centered in its proper position over the axle during all movements of bump and rebound, without any bump steer resulting from a linkage arm moving the outside wheel through a forced arc.

53

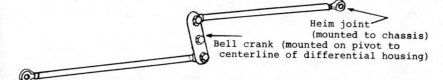

WATTS LINKAGE SET-UP

Heim joint
(mounted to chassis)
Bell crank (mounted on pivot to centerline of differential housing)

Heim joint (mounted to chassis)

PANHARD BAR

The full length Panhard bar is the simplest and most widely used of the lateral control linkage systems. It is attached to the chassis at one side of the car and attached to the axle housing at the opposite side of the car. It is simply a long tube with spherical rod end bearings at each end which brace one side of the car against the other to result in no side shift of the axle.

A drawback of this system as compared to the Watts linkage is that it moves in an arc rather than straight up and down. The shorter the bar, the sharper the arc it scribes.

Using a full length bar which goes all the way from one side of the chassis to the other, the amount of arc it moves in is minimal if the wheel moves a normal distance into bump (up to 2½ inches). With more bump travel, however, the increased arc of the bar will begin producing significant bump steer.

The same problem is present with a short Panhard bar. We have seen many applications of a Panhard bar which mounts to the rear end housing center section and is attached to the chassis on its outside. The sharp arc of the short bar as compared to the smoother arc of the wheel it is controlling results in bump steer of the rear wheel.

The mounting of the Panhard bar is extremely important. First, it should be mounted parallel to the axle and to the ground. If the bar were to be mounted at an angle, its arc would be moving in a direction against the natural bump arc of the outside wheel, creating bump steer by forcing the whole axle toward the outside of the turn.

It is extremely important the bar be straddle mounted between brackets which are stiff enough for the application. Most people do not realize the extreme torque which is placed on the mounting brackets of the panhard bar. We have seen brackets completely ripped out of the frame rail because of improper mounting. The answer to this problem, which is being employed on many Grand National cars, is to triangulate the mounting bracket with a cross tube. See accompanying photo for clarification.

The bracket itself must be of at least quarter-inch thick material. If the bracket is not stiff enough, the outside wheel will experience deflection steer from the twisting of the bracket. Remember, the bracket may be strong enough, but still not stiff enough (meaning the bracket may be strong enough not to break but still be weak enough to allow twisting deflections).

JACOB'S LADDER

The Jacob's ladder is used to locate axles where the Panhard bar or Watts linkage is not practical. It can be installed in tight areas, yet if properly designed, its geometry will still yield the same effect in terms of bump steer that a long Panhard bar will.

The trick in designing the proper geometry of the Jacob's ladder is to not place the converging tubes at too severe an angle. The converging tubes, where their lines are projected to an instant center, form the effective length of the Panhard bar.

A Panhard bar mounted in a chassis with a triangulated brace.

A proper straddle-mounted Panhard bar.

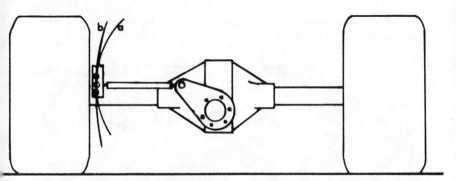

"A" is the arc scribed by the short Panhard bar illustrated. Compare the sharp arc of it to the smoother arc of a long Panhard bar, illustrated by "B."

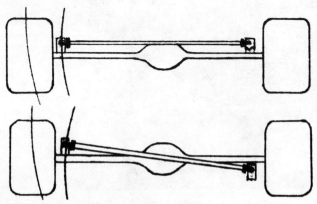

The top illustration shows the proper mounting angle of the Panhard bar parallel to the ground. Its movement arc is drawn in comparison to the movement arc of the wheel. The arcs are quite similar, and only slight bump steer will result. The bottom illustration shows what happens to the arcs when the bar is mounted at an angle. Considerable bump steer will result here.

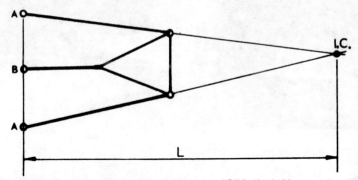

"A" marks the chassis mounts of the ladder arms. "B" is the ladder mount on the axle housing. "L" is the effective length of the ladder as a Panhard bar.

A Jacob's ladder installation on a modified. The angles of the arms are quite severe, resulting in a short Panhard bar effective length.

Another type of Jacob's ladder installation, this one being on a sprint car.

Anti-Squat And Anti-Dive

ANTISQUAT

Antisquat is the use of mechanical means to negate the squatting position of the rear of the chassis during acceleration.

The mechanical means is accomplished through the mounting points of the rear suspension linkage in relationship to the center of gravity height.

To determine the amount of antisquat present in a rear suspension system, a scale drawing of the side view of the car is made. A line is drawn from the center of the rear tire contact patch to the center of the pivot point which attaches the trailing arm of the axle to the chassis (or the instant center, if two trailing arms are involved).

This line is called the force vector. It is the force of the trailing arm acting on the chassis when acceleration is applied.

The force vector is projected past the center of gravity. If the force vector intersects the CGH, the car has 100 percent antisquat. If the force vector is located 50 percent of the distance between the ground and the CGH, the car has 50 percent antisquat. If the vector lies 20 percent of the distance from the ground to the CGH, there is 20 percent antisquat.

What the antisquat does is resist some of the downward squatting movement of the rear of the chassis when it is under accelerating

59

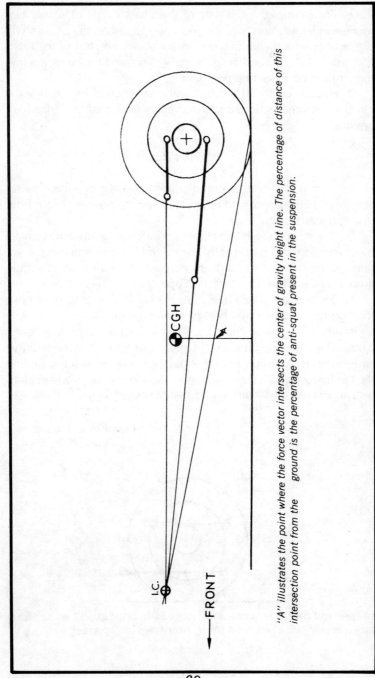

"A" illustrates the point where the force vector intersects the center of gravity height line. The percentage of distance of this intersection point from the ground is the percentage of anti-squat present in the suspension.

CGH

I.C.

◄— FRONT

force. For example, if the rear of the chassis dips or squats two inches under acceleration with no antisquat, then the chassis will dip only one inch with 50 percent antisquat. The rest of the loads that would be absorbed in spring deflection are now being fed into the suspension mounting points.

In general, up to 50 percent antisquat is good in a racing car chassis. Extreme antisquat causes rear wheel chatter under hard braking.

ANTIDIVE

Antidive is the same as antisquat except that it is a force vector employed in the opposite direction to keep the nose of the car from diving under braking loads.

The force vector is drawn from the center of the front tire contact patch to the instant center of the upper and lower A-arm line projections. If the force vector falls 25 percent of the distance from the ground to the CGH, the car has 25 percent antidive.

All percentages of antidive, from zero to 100 percent, have been tried on race cars and the best percentage seems to be zero.

Antidive creates too many problems in a race car. First, it creates caster change under braking loads. A large amount of antidive causes the front suspension pivot points to freeze up solid, turning the car into a go-kart with no suspension. This leads to wheel chatter and steering instability under heavy braking loads.

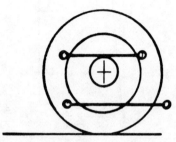

An upper and lower A-arm angle which runs parallel to the ground and parallel to each other will have an instant center at ground level and no anti-dive.

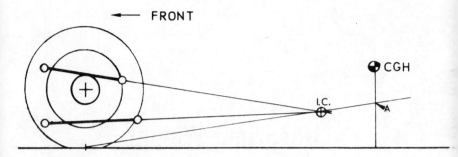

An illustration of anti-dive present in the front suspension. "A" is the point where the force vector crosses the center of gravity height line.

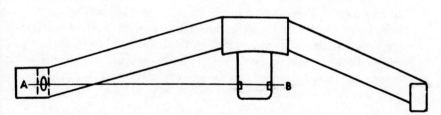

In a suspension system which utilizes a lower control arm and drag strut to form the lower A-arm unit, the inner mounting point of the drag strut must be in a straight line with the inner mounting point of the lower control arm (illustrated by the line from "A" to "B") in order to have no anti-dive in the suspension.

Unsprung Weight

Unsprung weight is the weight of suspension pieces which are not supported by the car's springs. Examples of these are tires, wheels, hub and spindle assembly, rear end housing and its contents, and brakes.

Suspension pieces which are hinged from the chassis contribute only one-half of their weight to unsprung weight. Because they are attached to the chassis, the other half of their weight is considered sprung weight. Components in this category include trailing arms, drag links, A-arms, leaf springs and the driveshaft. A torsion bar spring is completely sprung weight as it is a portion of the chassis.

On the adjoining page we have made a list of weights of components which go into making up unsprung weight on a stock car to help you determine the unsprung weight of your car.

HOW MUCH UNSPRUNG WEIGHT

It is desirable to keep unsprung weight to a minimum. The reason results from the frequencies it feeds into the springs. Unsprung weight suspension frequencies can be calculated just as sprung weight frequencies are, with the tire being the wheel rate.

The greater the mass of the unsprung weight, the lower the frequency. And the lower the frequency, the greater the amount of disturbance a bump on the road surface will have on deflecting the spring. Because the ideal situation is to keep to a minimum the amount that a road bump deflects the chassis, then if follows that the unsprung weight should be kept to' a minimum.

Unsprung weights

Component	Weight (in pounds)
Antiroll bar arms (each)	5*
Front coil springs (each)	17
Rear coil springs (each)	11
Floater rear end	133
Quick change floater	208
Tubular upper A-arms (each)	5*
Hub, spindles, backing plate assembly	35
Front brake drums (each)	35
Rear brake drums (each)	20
Chevy truck trailing arms (each)	28*
Ford lower A-arm with ball joint (each)	10*
Shock absorber (each)	4*
Grand National tire (each)	24
Grand National wheel (each)	24

*Denotes component whose weight only contributes one-half toward upsprung weight.

These weights were compiled from a 1974 Chevelle Grand National car with custom racing snout front end.

Wheel Rate

Wheel rate is the effective rate of a suspension spring at the center of the tire contact patch.

A spring rate in its straight pounds per inch of compression would only be effective at that rate if the center of the tire pushed straight down on the top of the spring. The farther away a spring is placed from the tire, the greater the leverage effect is on the spring, thus the weaker the effective spring rate becomes.

COMPUTING THE WHEEL RATE

The wheel rate is very easily found. The formula is "motion ratio squared times the spring rate equals the wheel rate." In the algebraic form we commonly use, that is expressed:

$$(MR)^2 \times K_S = K_W.$$

FINDING THE MOTION RATIO

For a coil spring which is compressed by the upward movement of a lower A-arm (for example, a Chevelle front suspension), the motion ratio is "distance number one divided by distance number

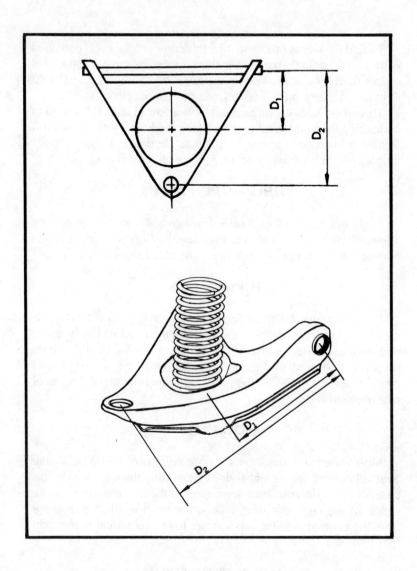

two." Distance number one (d_1) is the distance from the inner pivot point centerline to the centerline of the coil spring. Distance Number two (d_2) is the distance from the inner pivot point centerline to the lower ball joint centerline.

Let's take an example. Assume that d_1 is 8.5 inches and d_2 is 16 inches. D_1 divided by d_2 equals 0.531, which is the motion ratio.

To find the wheel rate, assuming this corner of the car is equipped with a 1,000 pounds-per-inch spring, square the motion ratio. This equals 0.282. Now multiply this answer by the spring rate (1,000 lb/in.), and the result is a wheel rate of 282 pounds per inch.

This wheel rate is a very important number to know. It is used in computing front end squat under braking loads, roll stiffness and roll stiffness distribution, spring frequencies, and many other chassis problems which we will encounter throughout this book.

OTHER MOTION RATIOS

There are many other types of suspension systems besides the one we have discussed above. Each one has its own way of determining the motion ratio. Each one is resolved separately below.

TORSION BARS

In cars equipped with torsion bars mounted parallel to the frame rails, such as in the Dodge and Plymouth, the motion ratio is one to one because the torsion bar is connected to the A-arm at the inner pivot point. Thus, d_1 and d_2 are the same length. So, a torsion bar's strength needs only to be the pounds-per-inch rating of the wheel rate required.

SOLID AXLE

Most American passenger cars are equipped with a solid rear axle with either coil or leaf springs supporting the car on it. In this case, d_1 is the distance from the center of the left rear spring to the center of the right rear spring. D_2 is the tread width (the distance from the centerline of the left rear tire to the centerline of the right rear tire).

MAC PHERSON STRUT

On the Mac Pherson strut suspension, and any double A-arm suspension using a coil spring-over-shock absorber unit, draw a line at a right angle (90 degrees) to the upright strut (or coil-shock unit) and project it straight to the inner pivot point of the lower A-arm. The length of this line is d_1. D_2 is the distance from the lower A-arm inner pivot point to the centerline of the arm's ball joint.

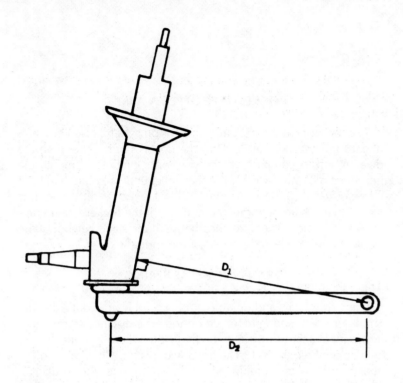

In both the Mac Pherson strut suspension, above, and the coil-spring-over-shock suspension, below, the motion ratio is figured the same way. D_1 is a line at a 90-degree angle to the spring-supporting upright and projecting to the center of the lower arm inner pivot point.

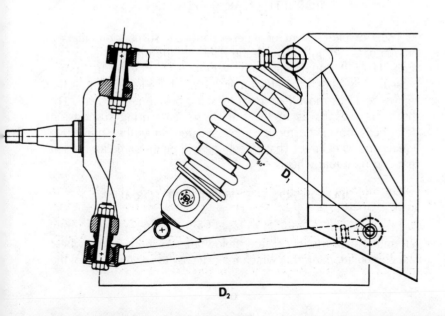

ROCKER-TYPE UPPER A-ARM

The rocker-type upper A-arm suspension system, also known as inboard front suspension, utilizes the upper A-arm rather than the lower A-arm to compress the suspension spring. To compute the motion ratio of this system, raise the wheel until the outer ball joint of the rocker beam raises one inch. This one inch is d_2. When d_2 is one inch, measure how much the inside of the rocker beam compresses the spring. The difference between the static heighth of the spring and this deflected heighth of the spring is d_1.

TRANSVERSE LEAF SPRING

Many sprint cars and modifieds use a solid beam front axle with a transverse leaf spring mounted on top. The distance from where the spring attaches to the axle on the left to where it is attached to the axle on the right is d_1. The tread width is d_2. When this motion ratio is squared and multiplied by the spring rate, the result is a single wheel rate. This is the wheel rate for both the left front and right front wheel because under body roll only one wheel at a time is being deflected.

CORVETTE REAR SUSPENSION

The Corvette system of independent rear suspension offers a unique case. To find d_2 move the right rear tire up into bump one inch. D_2 will equal one inch. When this wheel is in bump, measure how much the attachment point of the leaf spring at the right wheel has moved up from its static position. This is d_1. For the same reasons as in the transverse leaf spring suspension described above, the motion ratio squared times the spring rate equals one wheel rate. That wheel rate will be the same for the left rear and right rear wheels.

VARIATIONS OF THE WHEEL RATE FORMULA

Many times it is required to solve for the motion ratio or spring rate rather than the wheel rate. Below are variations of the wheel rate computation formula which make it easy to solve for any of the variables involved.

$$k_S \times (MR)^2 = k_W$$

$$K_S = \frac{K_W}{(MR)^2}$$

$$(MR)^2 = \frac{K_W}{K_S}$$

$$MR = \sqrt{\frac{K_W}{K_S}}$$

Shock Absorbers

The shock absorber's function is to damp out all the bumps and vibrations the chassis and wheel experiences. The input forces into the shock absorber come from the tires and the springs.

The amount of bump or vibration that a shock absorber experiences is measured in amplitude and acceleration. The main one we are concerned with here, in dealing with control, is the amplitude.

The amplitude is the heighth of the deflection force which the shock absorber experiences. A bump has a high amplitude and a low frequency compared to a vibration which has a low amplitude and a high frequency.

In order to control *all* of the vibrations as well as the bumps, the shock absorber must be mounted as close to the tire as possible. This is because the shock absorber rate is affected by the motion ratio in the same way a spring or antiroll bar arm is.

For example, the right front tire of a car experiences a vibration with an amplitude of one-half inch. If the lower A-arm length is 12 inches and the shock is mounted to the A-arm 6 inches to the inside from the ball joint, then the shock is only controlling 50 percent of the amplitude, or ¼-inch. This leaves ¼-inch of vibration free to nibble away at the tire's cornering power.

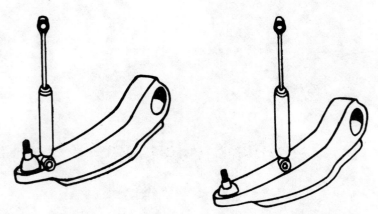

At left is the proper way to mount the shock absorber (as close to the ball joint as possible). At the right is illustrated the improper method of mounting a shock absorber.

SHOCK ABSORBER CONTROL

While shock absorbers do not affect the roll stiffness of a car, they can affect the springs' reaction to pitch and roll. To picture this, imagine driving a car into a hard corner with no shock absorbers at all attached. The roll and pitch will affect the car immediately, and because it is so immediate, the roll acceleration will cause the suspension to bottom-out. With shock absorbers attached, the roll will immediately slow down and be applied to the springs gradually.

A given car with a given weight, CGH and tread width, will always transfer the same amount of weight with a given G lateral acceleration, but the stiffness of the shock absorbers will slow or accelerate its roll and pitch action on the car.

The MoPar factory cars, above, employ an excellent method of mounting the shock absorbers. Bottom end is very close to the ball joint. The top end mounts very securely in a well triangulated hoop, making it an extremely rigid mount. On the car below, the rear shock absorber is properly mounted. The front shock absorber does little to control the small wheel bumps and vibrations. Its major purpose is to keep the nose of the car glued to the track on a superspeedway straightaway. It is a 70/30 shock. Its mount is an eye welded to the top of the tubing—not too rigid.

GABRIEL RACING SHOCK SPECIFICATIONS

Part Number	Control Ratio Compression-Rebound	Stroke in Inches	Collapsed Length	Extended Length	Control
64001	30/70	8 3/8	14 1/4	22 5/8	soft
64002	30/70	10 7/8	16 3/4	27 5/8	stiff
64003	60/40	8 7/8	14 3/4	23 5/8	stiff
64004	50/50	8 3/8	14 1/4	22 5/8	very stiff
64006	50/50	10 7/8	16 3/4	27 5/8	very stiff
64007	70/30	10 7/8	16 3/4	27 5/8	medium
64008	70/30	8 3/8	14 1/4	22 5/8	medium
64009	50/50	6 1/8	12	18 1/8	soft
64010	50/50	6 1/8	12	18 1/8	medium
64011	50/50	7 7/8	13 3/4	22 5/8	medium
64012	50/50	7 7/8	13 3/4	22 5/8	soft
64013	50/50	10 3/8	16 1/4	26 5/8	soft

MONROE RACING SHOCK SPECIFICATIONS

Part Number	Control Ratio Compression-Rebound	Stroke in Inches	Collapsed Length	Extended Length	Control
12376	50/50	6 1/4	11 15/16	18 3/16	light
12377	50/50	6 1/4	11 15/16	18 3/16	medium
12378	50/50	6 1/4	11 15/16	18 3/16	heavy
12575	70/30	6 1/4	11 15/16	18 3/16	n.a.
12673	45/55	6 1/4	11 15/16	18 3/16	n.a.
12674	40/60	6 1/4	11 15/16	18 3/16	n.a.
12386	50/50	8 1/8	13 13/16	21 15/16	light
12387	50/50	8 1/8	13 13/16	21 15/16	medium
12388	50/50	8 1/8	13 13/16	21 15/16	heavy
12585	70/30	8 1/8	13 13/16	21 15/16	n.a.
12683	45/55	8 1/8	13 13/16	21 15/16	n.a.
12684	40/60	8 1/8	13 13/16	21 15/16	n.a.
12396	50/50	10 1/4	15 15/16	26 3/16	light
12397	50/50	10 1/4	15 15/16	26 3/16	medium
12398	50/50	10 1/4	15 15/16	26 3/16	heavy
12595	70/30	10 1/4	15 15/16	26 3/16	n.a.

The Antiroll Bar

The antiroll bar is a very important and essential part of a modern race car's suspension system. Its job is to help take some of the roll resistance away from the springs. In doing this it helps limit body roll and suspension travel during cornering, limits severe camber change during cornering, and allows a very easy method of adjusting roll stiffness and roll couple distribution.

How does an antiroll bar do its job? It is a torsion bar mounted transversely across the chassis. It only begins working when the car moves in that direction (that is, body roll from inside to outside). When the car's body rolls, it resists the roll. It does this by taking weight off from the inside wheel and placing it on the outside wheel, while keeping the roll angle to a minimum.

It does this job by deflecting the bar with equal amounts of force. For example, if 200 pounds of force were to be loaded down on the bar at the right front, to keep the bar flat 200 pounds of force would need to be placed upward against the bar on the left front to resist it.

USING THE ANTIROLL BAR

One of the most important uses of the antiroll bar is to help

75

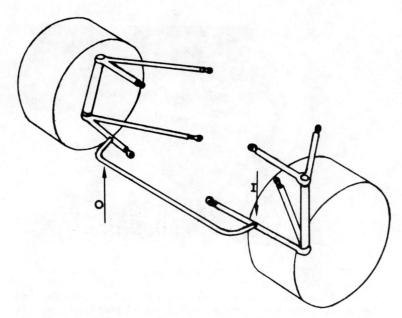

The antiroll is deflected by a load being fed in from the outside wheel and is resisted by the spring rate of the inside wheel.

balance the car for roll couple distribution. To illustrate how it works, let's suppose your car is understeering going into a left turn. Do you change to a softer right front spring, or change to a softer antiroll bar? The bar is easier to change, and is the best choice by far. The softer right front spring means the car is going to dive more (measured in inches) in the front when subjected to hard braking loads. If that should happen, the front wheels are subjected to more camber change because the wheels are traveling more in the bump position. It is far better to have the spring rates just stiff enough to resist the braking loads and let the antiroll bar resist body roll.

MOUNTING THE ANTIROLL BAR

Because the antiroll bar is resisting a great amount of torque, it is imperative that the bar be mounting extremely rigidly so its loads cannot deflect the frame rails it is mounted on, rather than the bar itself.

The best way to mount a bar is through a tube which is attached as a frame crossmember. The tube which carries the bar adds sub-

The bar in the photo above is mounted in aluminum blocks which clamp together over the bar. Note how far from the ball joint the bar is mounted onto the lower A-arm. This is undesirable, as will be explained at the end of this chapter. In the photo below, the bar is mounted in a bronze bushing clamped to the frame rails. Because of the clearance problems you can see which exist on the lower A-arm, the bar arm should have been mounted to the upper A-arm next to the ball joint for a more effective spring rate from the bar.

stantial torsional rigidity to the chassis structure. The accompanying drawing and photos illustrate how the roll cage should properly be triangulated to the antiroll bar attachment points for maximum rigidity.

If the bar is not carried in a tube, the next best method of mounting the bar to the frame is through holes cut through the frame rails. The size and strength of the frame rails add torsional rigidity to the structure to help resist the bar loading its torque into the chassis, and provide a convenient place for the roll cage to be triangulated into the frame rails above the bar.

The third alternative is mounting the bar in metal blocks which are bolted to the top of the frame rails. But the problem inherent in all ways of mounting is the amount of torsional rigidity available in the chassis to resist the torque twisting frame rails is limited to the strength of the bolts themselves. It also means the triangulation tubes of the roll cage must be mounted behind the mounting blocks instead of exactly on top of its center of action.

When choosing a tube or bushing size in which to carry the antiroll bar, choose a bushing of at least 1.5 inches diameter. This insures there will be sufficient room available should a large size antiroll bar be required.

THE BUSHINGS

When mounting the antiroll bar in any of the methods described above, it is important to have the bar mounted on brass bushings rather than rubber. A rubber bushing will stretch and deform, allowing the bar to slide around in its mounting and not be fully effective. A rubber bushing, completely deformed and twisted, could even cause the bar to become bound up in its mounting and not be able to twist at all.

A teflon bushing is nearly as bad as rubber. Teflon has a "cold flow effect," meaning it will stretch out of shape as force is applied to it.

HOW LARGE A BAR IS NEEDED?

The actual spring rate of the antiroll bar required is computed in examples in the "Computing Spring Rates" chapter found elsewhere in this book.

What is important here, however, is knowing how to compute bar size from spring rate required.

There are three variables involved in finding the spring rate of an

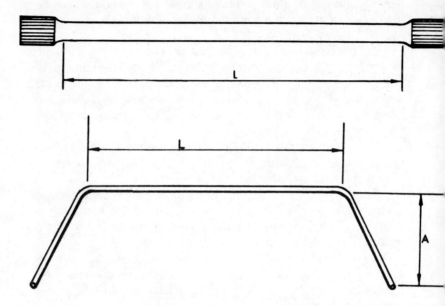

In both cases, "L" is the effective length of the bar. "A" in the lower drawing is the proper measurement technique to obtain the effective length of the arm when it runs at less than a 90-degree angle to the bar.

antiroll bar: 1) the effective length of the bar, 2) the effective length of the antiroll bar attachment arm, and 3) the diameter of the antiroll bar along its effective length.

The effective length of the antiroll bar is not necessarily the entire length of the bar. For example, a bar may be 38 inches long with two inches on each end of the bar reserved for the spline where the arm attaches and the journal where the bar rides on the bushings. Its diameter at the journals is 1.25 inches. Inside these two inches on each end the bar is turned down to a one inch diameter. The length of this smaller diameter inside the two bushing journals is the effective length of the bar because it is the only portion of the bar length which is subject to being twisted when the bar is loaded.

The effective bar arm length is the distance from the center of bar diameter to the center of the arm's attachment point to the A-arm on bars whose arms are mounted at a 90-degree angle to the bar. If the bar and arm is a one-piece unit, such as is used on almost all passenger cars, and the arm is mounted at less than a 90-degree angle to the bar, the effective length of the arm is the length of the arm as seen in the side view plane.

COMPUTING THE RATE OF A BAR

The formula for computing the rate of the antiroll bar spring rate is derived from the formula for determining the degrees of deflection of a round-shaped bar of metal. That formula is

$$\theta° = \frac{TL(57.295)}{JG}$$

θ is the Greek symbol theta which generally is the mathematical symbol for the degrees of an angle. In this case theta stands for the degrees of deflection. L is the effective length of the antiroll bar. G is the modulus of elasticity of the material. Antiroll bar material is generally 4130 or 4340, heat treated to Rockwell 33. In the case of this material, G equals 11,500,000 in our formula. J is the moment of inertia of the bar, which means the amount of force required to twist it in a circular motion. T is the effective bar arm length times the force (F), which is the unknown quantity in our equation for which we want to solve.

To help make the algebra easier in computing this rather complicated formula, we have rearranged the formula as J(G)(θ) = T (L)(57.295).

First we solve for the degrees of deflection. If the force rating we want is one which deflects the bar a certain amount in one inch travel of the arm (in other words, pounds per inch), then the degrees of deflection is the angle the bar arm travels to be moved upward one inch. A triangle can be constructed to picture the movement of the arm. The base of the triangle (the side adjacent to the angle) is the length of the bar arm. The side opposite the angle of the triangle is the one inch of movement. To compute the degrees of deflection, find the tangent of the opposite side (1) divided by the adjacent side (let's assume here the arm length is 12 inches in order to compute an example). So, 1 divided by 12 equals 0.0833. We look in the trig tables to find of what angle the tangent is 0.0833. It is 4° 47′, or 4.78 degrees. This number is substituted into the formula in place of θ.

Next we find the value of J. The formula for computing J is $\frac{1}{2}(\pi)r^4$. The value of π (pi) we use is 3.14. R is the radius, or one half of the diameter. The radius is taken to the fourth power (multiplied by itself four times). To figure an example, let's say the diameter of our bar is one inch. So, the radius (r) is 0.5 inch. J=.5(3.14) (.5)^4.

J=.098. Substitute this number into the formula for J.

The rest of the numbers for the formula are straightforward. G is 11,500,000. L is the effective length (let's assume for our example 23.5 inches). T is the arm times F, or 12 F for our equation.

To solve for F:

$$JG(\theta°) = TL(57.295)$$
$$(.098)(11,500,000)(4.78) = 12F(23.5)(57.295)$$
$$5,387,060 = 16157.19F$$

$$\frac{5387060}{16157.19} = F$$
$$333.4 = F$$

Our answer, 333.4, is the spring rate of the antiroll bar in pounds per inch. However, unless the bar arm is attached to the A-arm at the centerline of the ball joint, the bar is not effective at this full rate because of the leverage effect of the A-arm to which it is attached.

The motion ratio formula is applied to the antiroll bar spring rate just as it is with a suspension spring. The antiroll bar spring rate times the motion ratio squared equals the effective bar spring rate.

For our example, assume the lower A-arm is 19 inches long. This would be d_2. D_1 would be the distance from the lower A-arm inner pivot point to where the bar arm attaches to the lower A-arm (assume this distance is 15 inches). The motion ratio then is d_1 divided by d_2, or 15 divided by 19, which equals .79. The motion ratio squared is $(.79)^2$ or .6241. This number times the bar spring rate (333.4) equals 208 pounds per inch, or the effective bar rate.

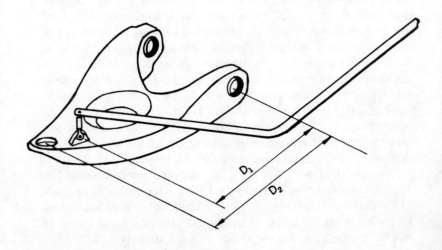

The anti-roll bar is mounted to the upper A-arm on the 1974 Penske Matador, above, so that the centerline of the mount is in direct line with the centerline of the ball joint. The result is that the motion ratio is 1.0, and the wheel gets the full benefit of the spring rate of the bar. The car in the photo below has a good strong mount, although it should have been moved to the right to be in line with the ball joint.

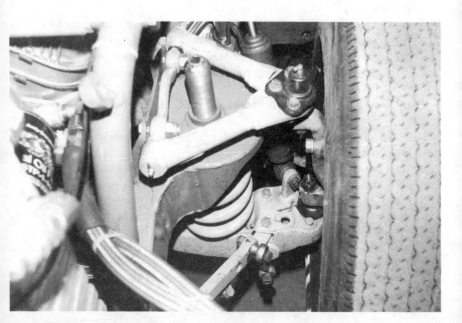

Spring Frequencies

Understanding spring frequencies is very important to the calculation of spring rates required for any application in a racing vehicle.

Because every type of racing vehicle varies greatly in regards to sprung weight, unsprung weight, motion ratio and weight distribution, the spring frequency is the only method available which will designate a particular spring requirement from a general formula.

THE BASIC NATURE OF OSCILLATIONS

To understand a frequency, it is necessary to understand the basic nature of oscillations.

A periodic motion is one which repeats itself. An example is the up and down motion of a weight hanging on a spring. An oscillation is the period of time required for the spring to extend, compress past its starting point, then return to its original starting point.

A frequency is defined as the number of oscillations traveled in one second. For example, if one complete oscillation takes 1/10-second, then ten complete oscillations are performed in one second. The frequency of this example would be 10 cycles per second.

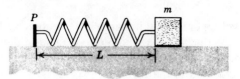

(a) Spring at rest with its natural length L.

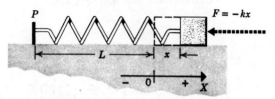

(b) Extended spring.

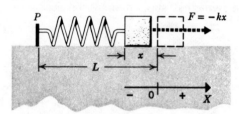

(c) Compressed spring.

To understand the relationship between the force of a spring and its frequency, consider a mass m sliding on a perfectly frictionless surface and attached to one end of a spring. The other end of the spring is affixed solidly to a peg. See accompanying drawing for clarification.

In drawing a the mass and spring are at rest (in the static state). The spring has a natural length L and it exerts no force on m. In drawing b, the mass has been given a displacement to the right (or in other words, forced to the right). This increases the length on the spring from L to $L+x$. It is a characteristic of a spring that when it is extended, it will immediately exert an opposite force in order to regain its original length. The greater the extension of the spring by the mass, the greater the restoring force. This restoring force, in fact, is directly proportional to the extension of the spring.

Once the spring exerts its restoring force, it will compress itself past its starting point into further compression, as seen in drawing c. After its compression at this point, it will again extend itself. When it goes past its starting point, the spring has made one cycle. How many of these cycles per second it makes is its frequency. And how many cycles per second it makes from one excitation depends directly on the exerting force of the spring (measured as its spring rate) and the mass connected to the spring.

CALCULATING THE FREQUENCY

There is a straightforward formula which can be used to calculate the frequency of any spring and mass system:

$$F_{cps} = .159 \sqrt{\frac{k_w}{M}}$$

K_w is the wheel rate of the spring in question. M is the sprung weight of the car which is supported by the spring in question divided by 384.

AN EXAMPLE

Let's calculate an example of spring frequency to see how it works. Our example car is a Grand National Chevelle. It has 732 pounds of sprung weight at the right front, and is equipped with a 1000 pounds-per-inch spring. The motion ratio squared is .335, so the wheel rate is 335 pounds-per-inch. 335 becomes the value of K_w in the equation.

If the sprung weight is 732, 732 divided by 384 equals 1.9. This is the value of M in the equation.

Working the equation out algebraically:

$$F_{cps} = .159 \sqrt{\frac{K_w}{M}}$$

$$= .159 \sqrt{\frac{335}{1.9}}$$

$$= .159 \sqrt{176.3}$$

$$= .159 (13.278)$$

$$F = 2.111_{cps}$$

Because automotive spring frequencies are most commonly expressed in cycles per minute, multiply the answer we found (which is in cycles per second) by 60 seconds. The answer is 126.6 CPM.

When we calculate spring rates for a car elsewhere in this book, we will demonstrate how to work this formula backwards to determine the spring rate required.

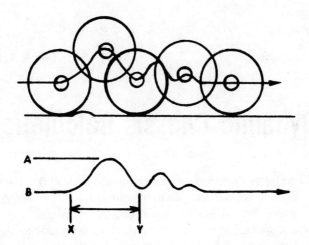

"A" to "B" is the amplitude of the frequency when the wheel hits a bump. "X" to "Y" is one cycle.

Dynamic Chassis Calculations

In order to determine what spring and antiroll bar rates are required, or to determine what specific area in the suspension is causing handling difficulties, it is necessary to make several dynamic chassis calculations in a specific order. These include total effective wheel rate force, roll couple distribution, static weight distribution, dynamic weight distribution, load transfer during cornering, total overturning moment, total roll stiffness, chassis roll angle, wheel deflection caused by body roll, and suspension frequencies.

If these calculations are carried out step by step and combined with the guidelines supplied in which each answer should fall, a thorough analysis of any racing chassis can be performed. This analysis will bring to light specific problem areas in a chassis.

EFFECTIVE WHEEL RATE FORCE

The effective wheel rate force is simply the total sum of all four wheel rates, plus the effective rate at the wheel of the antiroll bar(s). It is expressed in pounds-per-inch.

ROLL COUPLE DISTRIBUTION

Roll couple distribution is the expression (in a percentage) of how much body roll torque is resisted by the front springs and how much is resisted by the rear springs.

The more roll couple a pair of wheels resists, the greater the amount of weight transfer at that pair of wheels from the inside to the outside. This is the reason why racing vehicles must have a much higher roll couple or roll stiffness at the front.

To compute the roll couple for the front pair of wheels, add the front wheel rates and effective antiroll bar rate together and divide that sum by the effective wheel rate force. The answer will be in a percentage.

For most well-designed racing vehicles, the front roll couple will lie between 77 and 91 percent.

CENTER OF GRAVITY HEIGHTH

Center of gravity heighth (CGH) is needed to calculate several formulas in this book. How to find the CGH is covered in two of our books: "The Complete Stock Car Chassis Guide," and "Work Book for Advanced Race Car Suspension Development." We highly recommend that you have the Work Book in order to get more of this book. See page 172 for ordering information.

If you cannot calculate the CGH, a very close approximation is 15.5 inches for most stock cars, spring cars and super modifides.

ROLL CENTER HEIGHT

A racing vehicle's roll center height should be as low as practical so that lateral acceleration is transferred into body roll rather than lateral displacement at the outside tire's contact patch with the road.

As a rule of thumb for most well-designed front engine race cars, the front roll center should fall between ground level and three inches above ground level. The rear roll center should be slightly higher, falling between 4.5 inches above ground and 10 inches above ground.

The rear roll center should be higher so a greater proportion of weight transfer is taken at the front end of the vehicle in a turn.

ROLL AXIS TO CGH MEASUREMENT

Because a car rolls about its roll axis when it transfers weight from the inside to the outside during a turn, the distance from the roll axis to the CGH is what determines how much weight is transferred. The closer the roll axis is to the CGH, the less body roll there is. The less body roll there is, the softer the springs can be on the outside. But as we have pointed out, the higher roll centers promote higher lateral displacement at the outside tire contact patches, so it is much better to have more body roll and higher spring rates.

The front and rear roll centers determine the roll axis. The axis is simply an imaginary line drawn from the front roll center to the rear roll center through the centerline of the car.

Throughout the examples in this book where we have used the

formula:

$$\frac{W \times CGH \times G}{TW}$$

to calculate the amount of lateral weight transfer, we have used the CGH to be the distance from the ground to the CGH. We have done this just for the sake of clarity and brevity. To be absolutely correct when using this formula, the CGH figure should be the distance from the roll axis to the CGH. This is determined as the following diagram shows:

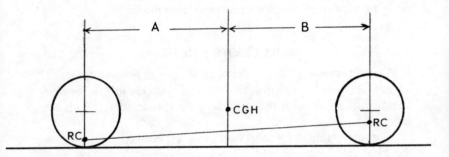

CGH_1 is the distance from the ground to the CGH
A is the wheelbase multiplied by the rear weight bias
B is the wheelbase multiplied by the front weight bias
RC_f is the front roll center height
RC_r is the rear roll center height
WB is the wheelbase

To work an example of this, let's examine a car with a wheelbase of 74 inches, a CGH_1 of 14 inches, a front roll center heighth of 2.5 inches, a rear roll center heighth of 4 inches, a front weight bias of 48 percent (.48) and a rear weight bias of 52 percent (.52).

A = 74(.52)
   = 38.48

B = 74(.48)
   = 35.52

89

$$CGH_1 - \frac{B(RC_f) + A(RC_r)}{WB}$$

$$= 14 - \frac{35.52(2.5) + 38.48(4)}{74}$$

$$= 14 - \frac{88.8 + 153.92}{74}$$

$$= 14 - 3.28$$

$$= 10.72''$$

These calculations help us to see why there exists such a wide variation in rear spring rates in stock cars. The lower the rear roll center height, the larger the moment arm acting between the roll axis and the CGH during body roll, thus creating a higher amount of overturning force which must be resisted with higher spring rates on the outside.

Rear roll center heights vary greatly among stock cars. They are determined by the spring anchorage height with leaf springs, so the roll center can be anywhere from 15.5 inches (with the leaf clamped onto the axle and using a high rolling radius tire) to 12 inches (a one-inch lowering block used with the leaf spring and a small rolling radius tire). With coil springs and a Panhard bar, the roll center is located at the point the Panhard bar crosses the car's centerline. If the panhard bar was mounted beneath the rear end housing, the rear roll center on this type of car could be as low as 7.5 inches.

STATIC WEIGHT DISTRIBUTION

The static weight distribution has to be calculated in two parts: total weight distribution and sprung weight distribution.

To determine the total weight distribution for a vehicle already constructed, simply weigh the vehicle on wheel scales or with a chassis checker.

To determine the total weight distribution for a vehicle in the design stage, the desired percentage of front-to-rear weight bias and left-to-right weight bias are determined in percentages.

Let's take an example to make it easier. Our design goal is a 3,800-pound Grand National stock car with 48 percent of the front-to-rear weight on the front wheels and 55 percent of the lateral weight on the left wheels.

First multiply the total weight, 3,800 pounds, by the front wheel percentage:

$$3,800 \times (.48) = 1,824$$

Next multiply this answer by the left wheels percentage:

$$1,824 \times (.55) = 1,003$$

This answer is the desired weight of the left front wheel. Subtract the left front weight from the total front weight, and the answer will be the right front weight:

$$1,824 - 1,003 = 821$$

For the rear weights, multiply the total weight of the vehicle by the rear weight–bias percentage:

$$3,800 \times (.52) = 1,976$$

Multiply this answer by the left side lateral weight bias:

$$1,976 \times (.55) = 1,087$$

The above answer is the left rear weight. Subtract the left rear weight from the total rear weight, and the answer is the right rear weight:

$$1,976 - 1,087 = 887$$

To determine sprung weight distribution, subtract the total weight of unsprung components at each corner of the car. For help in determining the unsprung weights of components, see the chapter on unsprung weight elsewhere in this book.

LOAD TRANSFER DURING CORNERING

To determine the load transfer during cornering, use the formula:

$$\frac{W_S (CGH\text{-}RC) \times G}{TW}$$

W_S is the total sprung weight. (CGH-RC) is the distance from the roll axis to the center of gravity height. G is the lateral acceleration. These three number multiplied together equals the **overturning moment**. When the overturning moment is divided by TW, the tread width, the answer is the amount of weight transferred from the inside to the outside during cornering.

TW, as used in this formula, is the average tread width. Many cars use a wider tread width in the front than in the rear. The two widths are added together and divided by two for the average tread width.

DYNAMIC WEIGHT DISTRIBUTION

The dynamic weight distribution is the distribution of the weight of the vehicle on its four wheels during a particular G turn.

To determine the front dynamic weight transfer, multiply the load transfer during cornering by the front roll couple percentage. The answer is the amount of weight added to the outside wheel. This same amount of weight is transferred from the inside wheel, so subtract it from the inside wheel static weight.

To determine the rear dynamic weight transfer, multiply the load transfer times the rear roll couple percentage. The answer is the amount of weight added to the outside wheel static weight. This same amount of weight is subtracted from the inside rear wheel.

ROLL STIFFNESS

Roll stiffness is the resistance of the sprung mass rolling about the roll axis, against the wheel rates of the vehicle trying to resist it.

Roll stiffness is measured in foot-pounds per degree. This is the foot-pounds of torque required to roll the car about its roll axis one degree. The higher the amount of roll stiffness a vehicle has, the higher the amount of weight transfer from inside to outside.

Front to rear roll stiffness distribution, expressed in foot-pounds per degree, is proportional to roll couple distribution (front to rear), expressed in a percentage.

CALCULATING ROLL STIFFNESS

The first calculation to be made in determining roll stiffness is the amount the outside wheels deflect upward when the body rolls about the roll axis one degree. This is done using the trigonometric function tan=opp/adjacent. We know already the angle is one degree and the adjacent side is one-half the tread width, so we are solving for the opposite side.

Next we have to know the total effective wheel rate force. This is simply the sum of all four wheel rates plus the antiroll bar effective rate.

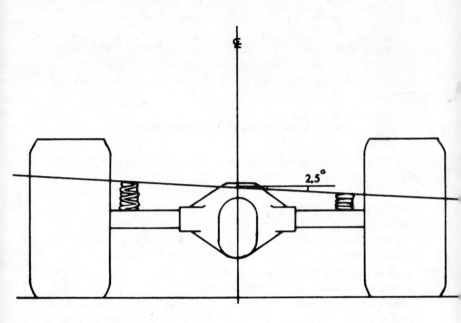

2.5°

If the vehicle rolls one degree, it has a force of one-half the total wheel rate force times the deflection pushing down on the outside springs. It also has the same force pushing up on the inside springs, so the total roll stiffness equals the total effective wheel rate force times the deflection times one-half the tread width. The answer will be in inch-pounds per degree. Leave it in this term rather than converting it to foot-pounds per degree.

Let's examine how this is calculated. Our example car has a total effective wheel rate force of 1,147 pounds per inch. The tread width is 62 inches, so one-half the tread width is 31 inches. The deflection of the right side, if rolled about the roll axis one degree, is

$$\tan 1° = \frac{x}{31}$$

$$.01745 = \frac{x}{31}$$

$$.01745(31) = x$$

$$.541 = x$$

So the calculations to determine the roll stiffness are:

$$31 \times 1,147 \times .541 = \text{roll stiffness}$$

$$19,236.3''/\#/° = \text{roll stiffness}$$

CHASSIS ROLL ANGLE

The chassis roll angle is the angle at which the body rolls about the roll axis during a specified lateral acceleration turn. This angle is in relationship to the level ground.

To determine the chassis roll angle, divide the overturning moment by the total roll stiffness. The answer is the angle expressed degrees. The roll angle for a stock car should not exceed 2.5 degrees. Cars which have less ground clearance should have smaller roll angles.

WHEEL DEFLECTION CAUSED BY BODY ROLL

When the body rolls about the roll axis at a specified angle, it is possible to calculate how much suspension travel on the outside wheels is used up by the springs resisting the body roll.

The formula used to determine this is:

$$M_{ot} - M_r = 0$$

M_{ot} is the overturning moment, which we have already calculated. M_r is the restoring moment, which equals one-half the tread width times the average wheel rate force, times x . The answer will be expressed in inches.

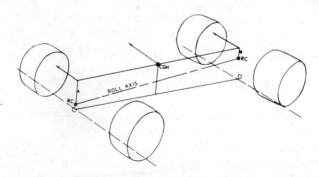

"A" is the distance from the front roll center to the CGH. "B" is the distance from the rear roll center to the CGH. The "roll axis to CGH" computation takes an average of these points all along the roll axis for a precise calculation of the rolling moment. The line from "C" to "D" is the ground plane.

Weight Distribution

For any racing vehicle, weight distribution should be at least 50 percent on the front wheels and 50 percent on the rear wheels. In stock car racing classes, it is possible to gain this distribution with careful construction (unless the rules are highly restrictive).

If the car is to be used on an oval track with left turns only, at least 55 percent of the left-to-right weight (lateral distribution) should be on the left side wheels. If a car is raced on tracks with both left and right turns, lateral weight distribution should be 50 percent on each side.

HOW MUCH WEIGHT AT THE REAR?

To plan how much weight should be placed at the rear of a car, the rule of thumb should be "the more, the better."

A car is able to accelerate faster coming off a corner with more weight bias at the rear. For a given amount of acceleration, the cornering force available on the inside tire increases tremendously when there is a heavier rear weight bias.

Braking ability is also enhanced with a rear weight bias. The more weight moved to the rear wheels, the more weight that remains there under heavy braking. And the best braking is achieved when the car's weight distribution, under maximum braking forces, is as close to 50/50 as possible. For example, we will consider a stock car weighing 3,800 pounds with a center of gravity height of 16 inches, a maximum braking potential of 1.1 G's and a wheelbase of 115 inches. The car will transfer forward 582 pounds of weight from the rear wheels onto the front wheels no matter what the car's weight distribution is. If the car had a static weight distribution of 52 percent on the front wheels and 48 percent on the rear wheels, under 1.1 G's of braking force the front wheels would have 67.3 percent of the vehicle's weight on them. If the car had a static weight distribution of 47 percent on the front wheels and 53 percent on the rear wheels, under 1.1 G's of braking force the front wheels would have only 62.3 percent of the total vehicle weight on them. What this shows us is that if 5 percent of the total vehicle weight can be statically placed on the rear wheels, it will remain there under any braking force. And in this case, 5 percent of the weight is 190 pounds—a very significant figure.

CGH VERSUS WEIGHT

The center of gravity height plays a significant role in determining the amount of rear weight bias that is practical. The lower the car's CGH, the more weight can be put on the rear wheels and still maintain maximum acceleration coming out of corners. This is because the CGH plays a major role in determining how much weight is transferred laterally in a turn. For example, if a car had a sprung weight of 3,000 pounds, a tread width of 60 inches and cornered at 1 G, it would transfer 800 pounds with a 16-inch CGH and 1,000 pounds with a 20-inch CGH.

Using this information along with the information contained in the chapter "Weight distribution versus roll couple distribution," it can be seen that to maintain the proper roll couple distribution, as little weight transfer as possible must take place at the rear wheels.

ACCELERATION AND BODY ROLL

The major asset of a heavy rear weight bias, as we have already pointed out, is in helping the car gain greater acceleration out of a turn. This is a situation where lateral acceleration is causing weight transfer to the outside, and yet as much thrust as possible is needed at the rear wheels to begin forward acceleration. The following diagram compares the advantage of a car with 55 percent of its total

96

weight on the rear to one with a 50/50 weight distribution. The results in example two point out that more forward thrust is available at the rear inside tire as compared to example one, and the car in example two will not be experiencing as much understeer because its outside front tire is not carrying as much weight.

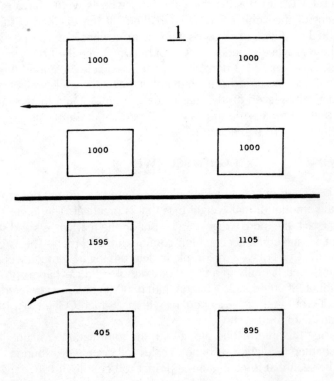

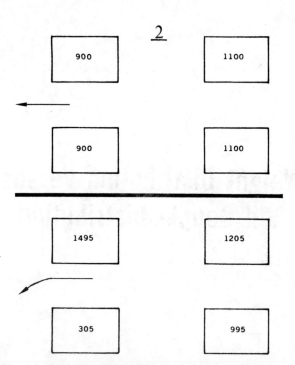

2

900	1100
900	1100

1495	1205
305	995

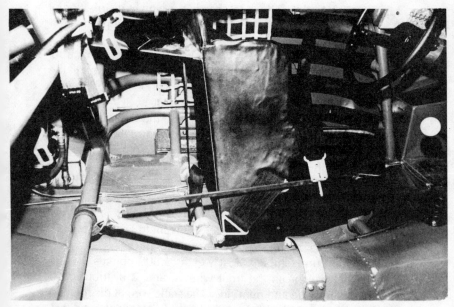

Notice the piece of ballast at the left of the driver's seat, situated outside of the roll cage. This is one method of gaining additional weight bias to the left side.

Weight Distribution Versus Roll Couple Distribution

Many people find it difficult to change the weight distribution of their race car because they do not know how to bring the roll couple distribution back into balance.

Assume you have a car which weighs 3,800 pounds with a front weight bias of 51 percent. In order to gain more acceleration off the turns with your car, you want to change the location of the ballast to give a net effect of 52 percent rear weight bias. If the car was perfectly balanced before making the change (no oversteer or understeer) with 85 percent front roll couple, how must the roll couple distribution be changed in order to keep the car in balance with the new weight distribution?

The *front* roll stiffness must be increased because, without changing roll couple distribution, the more weight that is put on the rear wheels, the more weight that will transfer to the outside rear tire. And this is what we want to minimize. We want to keep the weight as even as possible on the rear tires for traction.

To compute our example car, it weighs 3,800 pounds, has 51 percent of that weight on the front wheels, and is distributed 50 percent on the left side and right side. The static weight distribution then is 969 pounds on the left front and right front wheels, and 931 pounds on the left rear and right rear wheels.

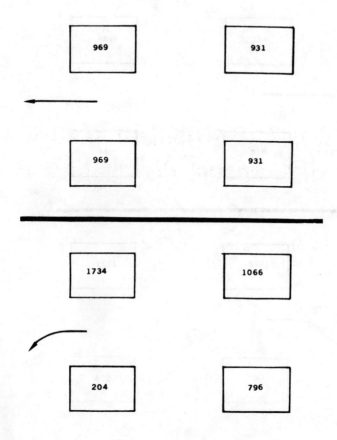

Example A

It has been calculated that the car transfers 900 pounds of weight from the inside to the outside through a 1 G turn. If the car has 85 percent front roll couple, it will transfer 900 pounds times .85 (or 765 pounds) at the front, and 135 pounds (900 times .15) at the rear.

So, the dynamic weight distribution of the car during a 1 G left hand corner is 1,734 pounds on the right front, 204 on the left front, 1,066 on the right rear and 796 on the left rear. (This is illustrated as example A in the accompanying diagrams.)

Now a new weight distribution (52 percent rear bias) is tried on the same car. The new static weight distribution is 912 pounds on the left front and right front wheels, and 988 pounds on the left rear and right rear wheels.

Under the same weight transfer—900 pounds—as before (no

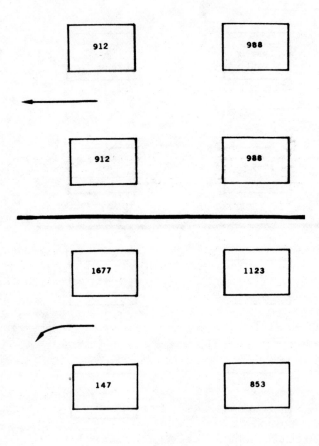

Example B

matter how the weight is distributed on the car, the total amount transferred from left front to right front stays the same), the dynamic weight distribution with 85 percent front roll couple under 1 G cornering is 1,677 pounds on the right front, 147 pounds on the left front, 1,123 on the right rear and 853 on the left rear. (This is illustrated as example B in the accompanying diagrams.)

Comparing the dynamic cornering weight distribution of example A to example B, the right rear tire of B is more heavily loaded by 57 pounds. If the car set-up in example A was a perfect balance—no oversteer or understeer—then the set-up in B will oversteer because its right rear cornering capability is lower because it is more heavily loaded.

101

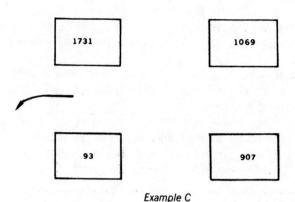

Example C

To balance the car, the front roll stiffness must be increased by adding a larger diameter anti-roll bar.

In order to get the same balance of dynamic weight on the outside tires in example B as in A, the front roll couple must be increased to 91 percent. This was determined by trying various higher values of front roll couple percentage until the outside tire weights in B matched those in A. The new dynamic weight distribution is 1,731 on the right front, 93 on the left front, 1,069 on the right rear and 907 on the left rear.

What we are trying to do is balance the amount of weight on the left rear and right rear tires so there is as little weight transfer to the right rear as possible during cornering. Of course this can be done with a 100 percent front roll couple (all of the weight will be transferred at the front and none at the rear). But this will make the right front tire much too heavily loaded and the car will understeer. So a compromise situation must be reached. The front roll couple distribution is backed off from 100 percent just enough so that the front end will not understeer.

THEORETICAL HANDLING LINE

From the information we have computed above, a theoretical handling line can be constructed. This is a graph showing that for any front weight bias, what the correct front roll couple distribution should be.

All that need be known is the correct front roll couple distribution for two different values of front weight bias. A graph is drawn with the x axis being the percent of front roll couple and the y axis being the percent of front weight bias. Plot the two values of each of the two situations we have computed. Draw a straight line between the two dots and extend the line all the way from the y axis to the x axis.

Working from this line, called the theoretical handling line, the correct amount of front roll couple can be chosen for any amount of front weight bias, or vice versa.

It must be noted, however, that these computed values are just a good starting point. Because of other factors which may enter into the handling scene, a change to more or less front roll couple may be required once the car is tested on the race track.

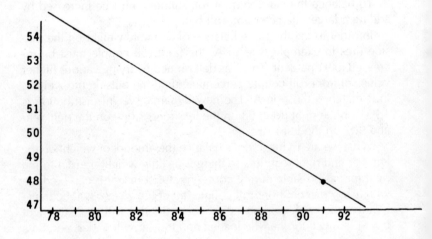

The inside front wheel on both the Porsches we see above is completely lifting off the ground. This indicates the front end of the vehicle is experiencing a 100 percent weight transfer and the chassis of the car is stiff enough that it will not flex under these conditions.

Acceleration And Deceleration Weight Transfer

BRAKING AND DECELERATION

Important to the selection of front spring rates, brake proportioning and camber change curve is the computation of how much weight is transferred from the rear of the car to front under braking loads.

The formula used to compute this is

$$\frac{W_t \times CGH \times G}{WB}$$

W_t is the total weight of the vehicle. CGH is the center of gravity height. G is the deceleration force. WB is the car's wheelbase.

To obtain the deceleration G's, some testing of the car must be done to compute it. Any long straightaway where the car can build up speed then decelerate with maximum braking force can be used. The data needed to be collected is the speed the car is traveling when it begins braking and the distance the car requires to stop.

The formula for computing this is

$$\frac{V^2}{2d} = \frac{a}{32}$$

V is the velocity, expressed in feet per second. To convert miles per hour into feet per second, multiply the miles per hour by 1.47. D is the distance in which the car stopped. A is the acceleration rate, or in this application of the formula, the deceleration rate (which is expressed in G's).

Let's take an example. We have a Grand National stock car with the total weight of 3,805 pounds. The unsprung weight is 635 pounds, so the total sprung weight is 3,170 pounds. The CGH is 16 inches and the wheelbase is 115 inches.

In testing the car on a straightaway for its maximum braking potential, we find that it stops from 75 miles per hour in 180 feet.

First, to compute the deceleration G's, 75 miles per hour times 1.47 equals 110.25 feet per second (the velocity). The velocity squared equals 12,155 feet per second per second. This is divided by two times the distance (2 x 180) or 360 feet. The answer is 33.764. Divide this by 32 (the constant of gravity), and the answer is 1.055 G's. This, by the way, is a good deceleration rate for such a massive vehicle. About the best deceleration G's we know of attained by a stock-type race car is 1.15 G attained by Herb Adams' Trans Am Tempest and Firebird, and similar rates by other Trans Am cars.

This problem above worked algebraically looks like this:

$$V = 75 \text{ mph} \times 1.47$$

$$V = 110.25$$

$$\frac{V^2}{2d} = \frac{a}{32}$$

$$\frac{(110.25)^2}{2(180)} = \frac{a}{32}$$

$$\frac{12,155}{360} = \frac{a}{32}$$

$$33.764 = \frac{a}{32}$$

$$\frac{33.764}{32} = 1.055$$

To compute the braking weight transfer, the total sprung weight (3,170) times the CGH (16) times the deceleration G's (1,055) equals an overturning moment of 53,509.6 inch pounds. This overturning moment divided by the wheelbase (115 inches) equals a frontward weight transfer of 465 pounds under 1.055 G's of deceleration.

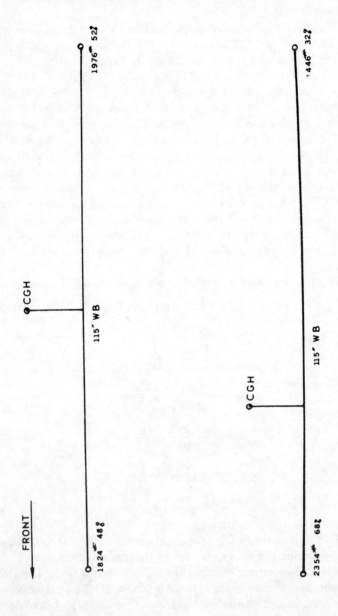

FRONT

CGH

115″ WB

1976″″ 52⅝

1824″″ 48⅞

CGH

115″ WB

1446″″ 32⅝

2354″″ 68⅝

107

This problem above worked algebraically looks like this:

$$\frac{W_t \times CGH \times G}{WB} = \text{transfer weight}$$

$$\frac{3{,}170 \times 16 \times 1.055}{115} = TW$$

$$\frac{53{,}509.6}{115} = TW$$

$$465 = TW$$

If this car's 3,805 pounds of weight were distributed 50 percent on the front wheels and 50 percent on the rear wheels statically, what would the new weight distribution be under 1.055 G's of deceleration? First of all, let's compute the static front and rear weight distribution. The weight of 3,805 times 50 percent (.50) equals 1,902.5 pounds. This would be the amount of weight on both of the front wheels combined and on both of the rear wheels combined.

If 465 pounds were transferred forward, they would be subtracted from the rear wheels and added to the front wheels. So, 1,902.5 minus 465 equals 1,437.65 pounds on the rear wheels combined. 1,902.5 plus 465 equals 2,367.5 pounds on the front wheels combined.

To compute the new weight distribution, 2,367.5 divided by 3,805 equals 0.622, or 62.2 percent of the total vehicle weight on the front wheels. 1,437.5 divided by 3,805 equals .378, or 37.8 percent of the total vehicle weight on the rear wheels.

This is a great demonstration of why so much more braking effort is required by the front wheels.

FRONT SPRING DEFLECTION

If 465 pounds of weight were transferred forward under 1.055 G's of braking, how much would the front springs deflect (compress)? This amount, incidentally, would be the same number of inches that the front end of the car would dip.

To compute this, add the left front wheel rate to the right front wheel rate and divide that sum by the amount of weight transferred. The wheel rate is used here rather than the spring rate because the weight transferred is fed to the springs by the action of the front wheels moving upward.

Assume the wheel rates of our car are 240 for the left front and 320 for the right front. The sum is 560 pounds per inch. Dividing that sum by the weight transferred, 465 pounds, equals 1.2 inches.

This spring deflection assumes there is no antidive present in the suspension linkages. If there was a percentage of antidive present in the geometry, how would this be figured?

Assume we have calculated 30 percent antidive in the car. 1.2 inches of spring deflection times .30 (30 percent antidive) equals .36 inches. 1.2 inches minus 0.36 inches equals 0.84 inches. This is the amount the springs would deflect with 30 percent antidive. What happens to the rest of the transfer load that was once 1.2 inches of deflection? The rest of the loads that would be absorbed in spring deflection are now being fed into the suspension mounting points.

ACCELERATION

Acceleration and weight transfer caused by it is figured exactly the same way that deceleration and braking weight transfer is.

The amount of weight transferred to the rear wheels under any amount of acceleration can be calculated with the formula

$$\frac{W_t \times CGH \times G}{WB}$$

W_t is the vehicle's total sprung weight. CGH is the center of gravity height. G is the acceleration force expressed in gravities. WB is the wheelbase.

To compute the acceleration G's, use the formula

$$\frac{V^2}{2d} = \frac{a}{32}$$

Assume a car accelerated to 75 MPH in a distance of 180 feet. 75 MPH times 1.47 equals 110.85 feet per second. That number squared equals 12,155. That answer divided by two times 180 feet equals 33.764. Dividing that answer by 32 equals an acceleration rate of 1.055 G's.

This problem above was worked using the same number values as the similar problem in the deceleration chapter to show that acceleration and deceleration rates and weight transfers are figured exactly the same way.

The amount of antisquat at the rear under acceleration would also be computed in the same manner as antidive was computed for the front end.

Calculating Spring Rates

Using the information and calculations we have already discussed, establishing the correct spring rates and anti-roll bar rate is a relatively easy process.

The easiest case to discuss is for a flat or very slightly banked track. To calculate the wheel rates required, use the spring frequency (or suspension frequency) formula. For the outside front wheel, the frequency should be 2 cycles per second for all front engine racing vehicles. For the outside rear wheel, the frequency should be 1.416 cycles per second on all front engine racing vehicles. Using these frequencies in the formula, solve for the wheel rate. Once the wheel rate is established, the wheel rate is divided by the motion ratio squared to convert it into spring rate.

The inside rear spring rate should be the same as the outside rear. The inside front spring rate should be 15% lighter in rate than the outside front spring.

Now that the spring rates are established, the anti-roll bar rate has to be calculated. First, compute the overturning moment (sprung weight times the roll axis to CGH distance times the G force). The G-force should be assumed to be 1.2 G's for all flat asphalt tracks.

Next, we want to find out what the roll stiffness torque is when the car rolls two degrees about the roll axis. Stock cars should not roll more than two degrees, and unlimited type race car with less

111

ground clearance should roll even less to prevent bottoming-out. To do this, use the formula

$$\frac{\text{overturning moment}}{\text{roll stiffness}} = 2°$$

and solve for the roll stiffness.

The roll stiffness torque must be converted into the total effective wheel rate required. Then the sum of the four wheel rates which have already been calculated are subtracted from the total effective wheel rate required to determine the anti-roll bar rate required.

To convert the roll stiffness torque into total effective wheel rate required, use the formula

$$(TW)\ (D)\ (.5X) = \text{roll stiffness}$$

and solve for x. TW is the tread width. D is the deflection of the wheels when the chassis is rolled about the roll axis one degree (the tangent of one degree equals the deflection divided by one-half the tread width—solve for the deflection).

The total effective wheel rate required minus the sum of the four wheel rates calculated from the spring frequencies equals the spring rate of the anti-roll bar required.

AN EXAMPLE

Let's determine the spring rates for a car which weighs 3,805 pounds, has a tread width of 62 inches, will corner at 1.2 G's on a flat track, and has a roll axis to CGH distance of 11.6 inches. Its sprung weight is 3,171 pounds, distributed 732 at the right front, 911 at the left front, 678 at the right rear and 850 at the left rear.

1) Spring frequency at right front:

$$2 = .159\ \frac{\sqrt{k}}{\sqrt{M}}$$

$$(M = \frac{732}{384} = 1.9)$$

$$2 = .159\ \frac{\sqrt{k}}{\sqrt{1.9}}$$

$$2 = .159\ \frac{\sqrt{k}}{1.378}$$

$$2\ (1.378) = .159\ \sqrt{k}$$

$$2.756 = .159\ \sqrt{k}$$

$$\frac{2.756}{.159} = \sqrt{k}$$

$$17.333 = \sqrt{k}$$

$$(17.333)^2 = (\sqrt{k})^2$$

$$300 = K$$

2) Spring frequency at right rear:

$$1.416 = .159 \frac{\sqrt{k}}{\sqrt{m}}$$

$$(M = \frac{678}{384} = 1.766)$$

$$1.416 = .159 \frac{\sqrt{k}}{\sqrt{1.766}}$$

$$1.416 = .159 \frac{\sqrt{k}}{1.329}$$

$$1.416 (1.329) = .159 \sqrt{k}$$

$$1.88 = .159 \sqrt{k}$$

$$\frac{1.88}{.159} = \sqrt{k}$$

$$11.823 = \sqrt{k}$$

$$(11.823)^2 = (\sqrt{k})^2$$

$$140 = K$$

3) Left front wheel rate =
   $300 \times .15 = 45$
   $300 - 45 = 255$
   255 is the left front wheel rate

4) The left rear wheel rate will be the same as the right rear (140), so the sum of the four wheel rates is:

   300 — right front
   255 — left front
   140 — right rear
   <u>140</u> — left rear
   835 — total

5) overturning moment

$$W_s \times (\text{CGH to Rt}) \times G =$$
$$3171 \times 11.6 \times 1.2 = 44.140$$

6) Roll stiffness

$$\frac{\text{overturning moment}}{\text{roll stiffness}} \quad 2°$$

$$\frac{44,140}{R} = 2$$

$$44,140 = 2R$$

$$\frac{44,140}{2} = R$$

$$22,070 = R$$

7) Converting to total effective wheel rate

$$\text{Deflection} = \tan 1° = \frac{x}{31}$$

$$.0175 = \frac{x}{31}$$

$$.0175 (31) = x$$

$$.543 = x$$

$$(TW) (D) (.5x) = \text{roll stiffness}$$

$$(62) (.543) (.5x) = 22,070$$

$$16.833x = 22,070$$

$$x = \frac{22,070}{16.833}$$

$$x = 1311$$

8) Anti-roll bar rate

```
  1311 (total effective wheel rate)
-  835 (sum of wheel rates)
   476 (rate of anti-roll bar required)
```

9) Roll couple distribution

```
   300 (right front wheel rate)
   255 (left front wheel rate)
   476 (anti-roll bar rate)
  1031 (total front wheel rate)
```

$$\frac{1031}{1311} = .786, \text{ or } 78.6\% \text{ front roll couple}$$

114

Banking Angle Corrections
For Spring Rates

BANKED TRACK ADJUSTMENT

For banked race tracks, an adjustment must be made to compensate for the additional down force the car generates. This is because the banking angle converts some lateral acceleration into down force. The steeper the banking, the greater the down force the car generates. How to compute the cornering G's of the banking angle is explained in the following chapter.

First, how many pounds of down force the car will generate must be computed. Divide that down force by four (because each of the car's four wheels will share equally in resisting the down force). Divide this answer by the car's total weight and the final answer is the number of G's of additional cornering force to which each wheel will be subjected.

Use this cornering G-force in the cornering weight transfer formula to determine how much additional weight in pounds will be added to the outside wheel's sprung weight. The same amount of weight will be added to each of the outside corners of the car.

Add this amount of down force weight to the sprung weight of the outside front and rear corners and refigure the spring frequencies with the same cycles per second as before (2 CPS at the front and 1.416 CPS at the rear). This will tell you what the new wheel rates should be for the outside corners on the banked track. The inside front should be 15% lighter in rate than the outside front, and the inside rear should be the same as the outside rear.

The anti-roll bar rate should stay the same as originally computed for the first trial on the track. The bar rate may then need to be changed slightly to correct for any over or under steer in the car.

AN EXAMPLE

We will compute the new wheel rates required for the same car as we began with in the previous example, this time with the car being raced on a track with 12-degree banking. The total amount of down force the car generates is 5,676 pounds. How this amount of down force is computed is used as an example in the chapter which explains calculating the down force.

1) Downforce G's:

$$\frac{5,676}{4} = 1,419 \text{ pounds per wheel}$$

$$\frac{1,419}{3,800} = .373 \text{ G}$$

2) Cornering weight transfer per outside wheel:

$$\frac{(3171)\,(11.6)\,(.373)}{62} = 221 \text{ pounds}$$

3) New sprung weights:

right front — 732
          221
          ‾‾‾
          953

right rear — 678
          221
          ‾‾‾
          899

4) New wheel rates:

right front —
$$2 = .159 \frac{\sqrt{k}}{\sqrt{\frac{953}{384}}}$$

$$393 = K$$

right rear —
$$1.416 = .159 \frac{\sqrt{k}}{\sqrt{\frac{899}{384}}}$$

$$186 = K$$

left rear — 186 = K

left front — 393 × .15 = 59

393 − 59 = 334

334 = K

A HELPFUL HINT

In actual practice, we have found that it is not necessary to correct for the banking angle until the bank is at least 15 degrees on a half-mile or longer track. The wheel rates which are calculated for the flat track are sufficiently stiff for most all banking angles on any track under a half-mile, and up to 15 degrees on a half-mile or longer. This is because the amount of downforce a car generates on a bank depends entirely on the car's speed on that bank. If the right front wheel bump travel is any more than 3 inches in the turns, then stiffer springs must be computed.

COMPUTING BANKING DOWN FORCE

To compute the downforce a car generates on a banked track, three things must be known: 1) the bank angle (which can be measured with an inclinometer), 2) the distance the car travels in a turn, and 3) the number of seconds the car requires to travel through a full turn. From (2) and (3), the turn radius can be computed.

The first step is to calculate the centrifugal force. Use the formula

$$CF = \frac{M\ (V^2)}{r}$$

M is the weight of the car divided by 32. V is the velocity in feet per second (the distance traveled divided by the number of seconds required to travel it). R is the turn radius.

Next, a resultant vector is figured. Use the formula

$$R = \sqrt{a^2 + b^2}$$

R is the resultant we want to solve for. A is the total weight of the car. B is the centrifugal force.

Once these three values are known, a scale drawing must be made. The most convenient scale is one inch equals 1000 pounds. If the centrifugal force is 6800 pounds its line would be drawn 6.8 inches long.

Draw the centrifugal force and total vehicle weight vector lines perpendicular to each other. The resultant line (labeled "R") is

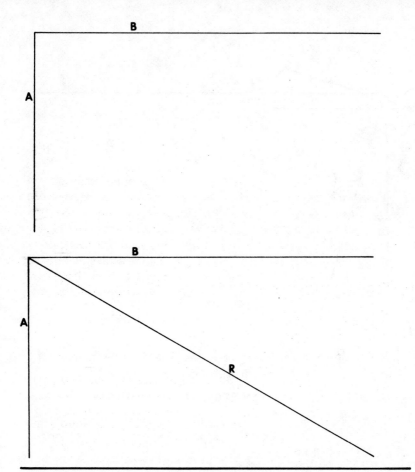

drawn at a 45-degree angle to either of the first two lines.

At this point, the banking angle is drawn in just below the origin intersection of the three existing lines. The origin intersection represents the center of gravity height of the car on the bank.

From the CGH, draw a line straight down at a 90-degree angle to the bank. This line will be called "C." Measure with a protractor the angle between lines "C" and "R."

First, the lateral force is figured. Use the formula

$$\sin \emptyset° = \frac{x}{r}$$

R is the value (in pounds) of the resultant. Solve for x.

Finally, the down force is figured using the formula

$$\tan \emptyset° = \frac{LF}{X}$$

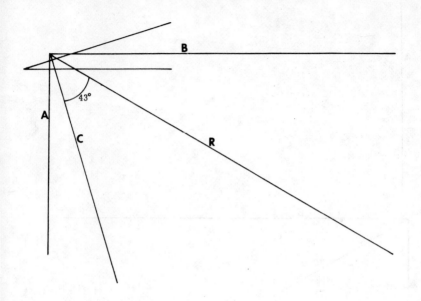

LF is the lateral force. Solve for x. The answer is the number of pounds of down force the car will generate.

AN EXAMPLE

We will examine a car which weighs 3800 pounds. The track it is running on has a 17-degree bank. The entire turn is 700 feet long. The car travels it in 6.2 seconds.

1) Radius

The formula for the circumference of a circle is $C = 2\pi r$. If the entire turn equals half a circle then C in this case equals two times the entire turn.

$$C = 2\pi r$$

$$2 \times 700 = \pi r$$

$$1400 = 2 (3.14) r$$

$$\frac{1400}{6.28} = r$$

$$223 = r$$

2) Centrifugal force

$$CF = \frac{(V^2)}{r}$$

$$= \frac{3800}{32} = 118.75$$

119

$$V = \frac{700}{6.2} = 113 \text{ FPS}$$

$$= \frac{118.75 \ (113)^2}{223}$$

$$= \frac{118.75 \ (12769)}{223}$$

$$= 6800 \text{ pounds}$$

3) Resultant

$$R = \sqrt{a^2 + b^2}$$
$$(a = 3800, \ b = 6800)$$

$$R = \sqrt{3800^2 + 6800^2}$$

$$R = \sqrt{1440010 + 46239980}$$

$$R = 7790$$

4) Scale drawing

$\Phi°$ between C and R = 43°

lateral:

$$\Phi = 43°$$

$$\sin 43° = \frac{X}{7790}$$

$$.682 = \frac{X}{7790}$$

$$.682 \ (7790) = X$$

$$5313 = X$$

down:

$$\Phi = 43°$$

$$\tan 43° = \frac{5313}{X}$$

$$.936 = \frac{5313}{X}$$

$$.936 \ X = 5313$$

$$X = \frac{5313}{.936}$$

$$X = 5,676 \text{ pounds}$$

Structural Stiffness

The race car structure receives extremely high loads which are fed into the chassis at the suspension and spring attachment points. Without a proper support of the chassis at these attachment points, the chassis will be twisted and deflected. This will cause a severe detrimental effect on the car's handling capability. Additionally, if the chassis members are continually subjected to these deflections, they will develop fatigue cracks. We have seen many such fatigue cracks on untriangulated sprint car frames and even on the massive Grand National stock car frames. These cracks have led to complete failure of main chassis frame members.

Engineers measure the rigidity of a chassis in terms of foot-pounds of torque required to deflect the chassis along its length one degree. If a chassis had a rating of 6,000 foot pounds per degree, for example, it would take 6,000 foot pounds of torque to deflect the chassis one degree.

This figure of 6,000 foot pounds per degree sounds like it might be high, but in reality, it is at the bottom of the scale for what is acceptable in a race car, especially a heavy car such as a stock car.

The average proven load factor of a race car subjected to normal pavement bumps is 3 G's download. Added to this should be a designed-in safety factor of 1.5 G's. For an example, a structure is

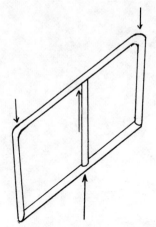 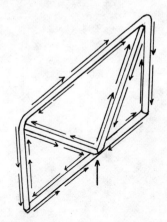

A comparison of two types of chassis structure, the left one untriangulated and the right one triangulated. The basic principle of triangulation is to spread the loads out evenly throughout the entire structure. In the right drawing, it is shown how a load fed in at the bottom center of the structure is evenly distributed throughout the entire structure. When the arrows of load distribution are pointing against each other on the same tube, this means the tube is accepting the load placed on it "in compression". In other words, the tube is literally trying to be compressed. This is its strongest asset. It resists compression and tension best, and bending the least. In the drawing at the left, all of the loads place the tubes in bending.

carrying 850 pounds of static load at the right front corner. At 4.5 G's, the structure is subject to 3,825 pounds of force. If that force is acting on the chassis through a point located 20 inches away from the suspension member's anchorage point, the torque the chassis is subject to is 3,825 pounds times 20 inches, or 76,500 inch pounds of torque. This is equal to 6,375 foot pounds of torque.

This amount of torque is being fed into the chassis at just one point. That point must be properly supported in order to spread this load out over a large area so that it does not overly stress one particular area and cause it to fail.

This is what triangulation is all about. A straight length of tubing, when subjected to this torque, will deflect (unless, of course, the tubing is of massive diameter and wall thickness). But if two other tubes were brought together in the shape of a triangle at the point the first tube was subjected to the torque load, that load would suddenly be spread out evenly over the three tubes, reducing the load factor on the first tube to one-third of the original amount.

The proper name for a structural frame constructed from tubing (including a roll cage constructed on top of a passenger car frame) is a space frame.

The photo above is a model of a basic space frame. Below is an engineer's model of the type of triangulation required to achieve a properly triangulated front bay for a stock car.

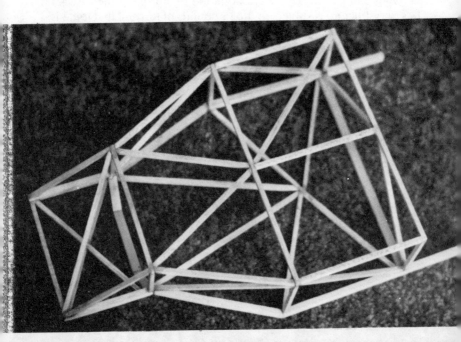

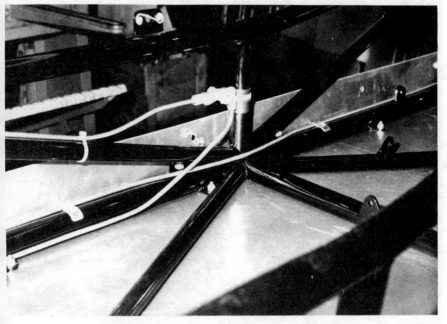

The joining of several tubes in a properly triangulated space frame.

A cardinal rule of thumb in space frame construction is that there must be a triangulated bay on each side of an untriangulated bay. In the typical front engine car, there are three bays: the engine compartment, the driver's compartment and the rear compartment.

Another rule of thumb for space frame construction is that all the loads fed into the chassis must place the frame members in tension or compression, and none in bending.

A third very important rule is to never run a tube into the middle of another tube without a third tube meeting it to form a triangulated junction. If two tubes are welded parallel to each other into a third tube at a 90-degree angle to the first two, without any triangulation, a moment arm will exist between the first two tubes acting to deflect the third between the attachment points.

The drawing on car number 11, above, illustrates the three types of forces imposed on a car in a corner which must be resisted by the chassis structure. "T" is the torsional stress. "S" is the shear stress imposed by lateral acceleration. "B" is the bending loads. The cage being constructed in the Datsun, below, is designed to properly withstand all of these loads. Notice how three different triangulated braces support the chassis where the spring loads are fed into it. The shear stress is resisted by the cross diagonal bracing. "X" bars will be built into the door spaces to resist bending loads.

A well-triangulated front bay of a stock car is shown above. In the photo below, notice the cross brace above the engine. This piece of tubing is one of the most critical components for proper bracing in the engine compartment.

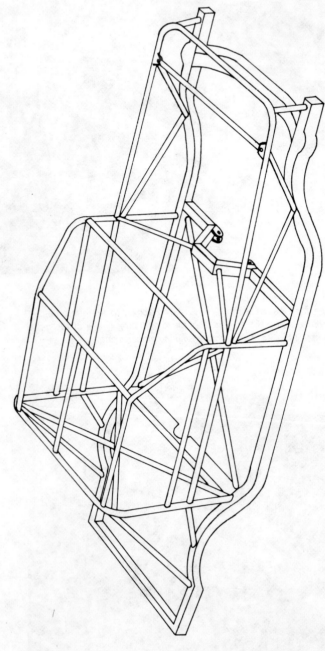

This illustrates a properly triangulated chassis structure for a NASCAR-type modified or modified-sportsman type of car. Not all of the door bars are included for sake of clarity.

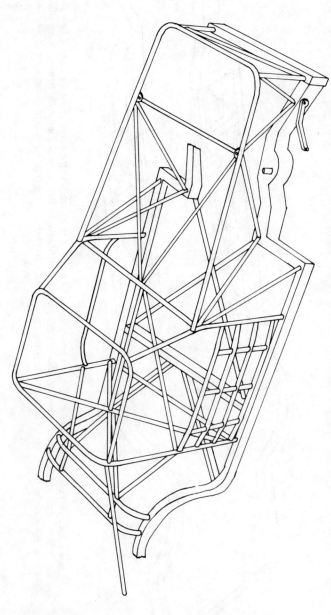

This is a properly triangulated chassis structure for a Grand National-type stock car. Notice the "X" brace in the bottom of the chassis below the driver's bay. This resists torsional and shear stress loads in the first and second bays. Not all of the door bars have been drawn in, nor has the frame been completed on the left side, for sake of clarity in the drawing.

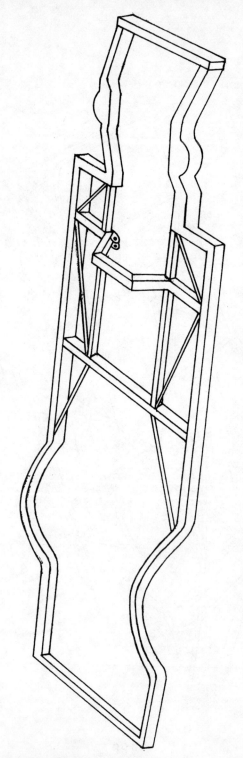

Sometimes driveline components make it impossible to place an "X" type of cross brace in the frame under the driver's bay. This type of bracing is an acceptable substitute. Notice the square tubing which constitutes the transmission-supporting frame crossmember. A cross piece is bolted in under the transmission to complete the crossmember. Additionally, the crossmember is triangulated above the roll cage.

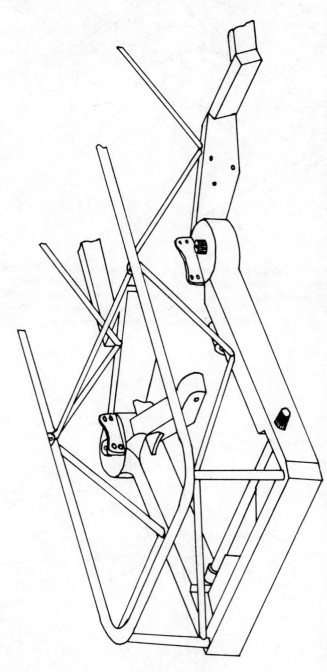

A detailed view of the proper type of triangulation required in the engine bay. Not shown is the cross brace which ties the lower A-arm mounting points together. This is a bolt-in piece to permit easy engine access.

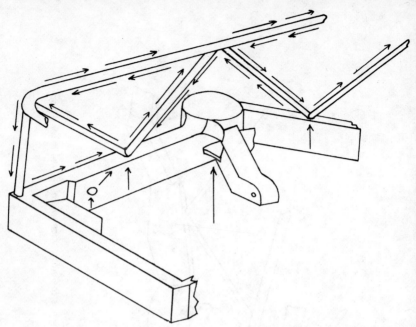

Above, the arrows indicate how a load fed in through the springs acting against the frame is fed into a properly triangulated chassis front bay. Notice that all of the tubes are completely straight with no bends or radii. Any bend will serve as a weak spot, allowing the structure to flex at that bend. Below, the arrows show how an untriangulated structure is flexed through bending loads imposed on it.

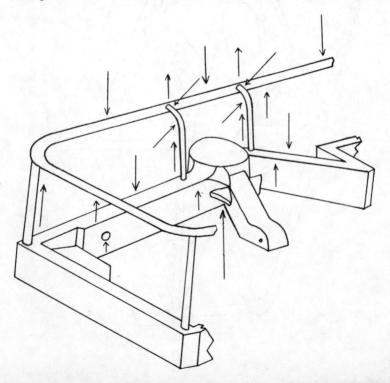

Another view of the Datsun, above, showing the proper triangulation of the middle and rear bays. Below, the front bay of the Datsun shows how the front spring loads are triangulated. After the engine is installed, a bolt-in cross brace will be added between the spring (strut) towers.

Above, a tube which is welded into the middle of another tube without a third tube to form a triangle will form a weak link in a structure. Feeding a load into the middle of the tube without triangulation will put the tube into a bending load, causing it to flex. And when that tube has a radius in it, as above, the tube is sure to flex with even light loads. Below, a view of an untriangulated front bay.

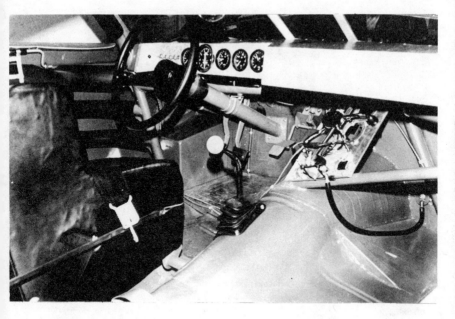

Above, a car with a square tubing transmission-supporting frame crossmember. Notice how the crossmember is triangulated from the roll cage. Below, a Dodge with a properly triangulated rear bay. The tubes have to support both the front and rear mounting points of the car's leaf springs so the frame rails are not flexed.

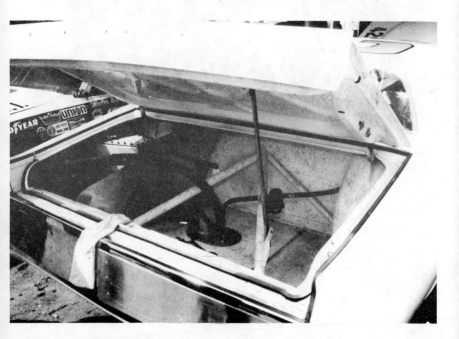

An A-arm with bends and curves in it, above, will not be nearly as strong as a straight triangular type, as shown below. Under heavy loading forces it turns and during braking, the curved A-arm will deflect, causing unpredictable wheel alignment changes.

A straddle mount for an A-arm, as shown above, is a very rigid type of mount. It is four times stronger than a control shaft bolted onto an upright plate. Its problem is in the adjustability of the A-arm for alignment changes. The one shown here must be removed from the chassis. The heim joint is screwed in or out to make a change. The only thing wrong with the set-up pictured here is the A-arm has a bend in it. The arms should be straight and the straddle mounts placed on an angle. Below is a bolt-in cross member between the inner mounting points of the lower A-arms.

CHECKING FOR STRUCTURAL STIFFNESS

It is possible for you to check the structural stiffness of any vehicle. To do this, remove the wheels and place the car on sawhorse-type supports. Place one support as far forward under the car as possible, and the other one as far to the rear as possible.

Attach a piece of roll cage tubing to the rear sawhorse level with the top edge of it. The tubing will run along the centerline of the car and protrude in front of it. The tubing provides the point about which the chassis will flex.

Move the front sawhorse out in front of the car and attach the tubing to it. The only support for the front of the car now is the tubing at the centerline of the car.

Attach another piece of roll tubing across the frame rails as close to the suspension mounting points as possible. Let this tube protrude at least 10 feet out to one side of the car.

Attach a third piece of roll tubing, equal in size to the second one, across the frame rails at back. It should protrude to the opposite side of the car from the front one. The purpose of this bar at the rear is to apply weight to the chassis to keep it anchored flat to the rear sawhorse.

At the front of the chassis, apply weight at the end of the 10-foot bar. Place an inclinometer on the bar above the point where it crosses the centerline of the chassis. Continue placing weight on the bar until the inclinometer shows a movement of one degree.

To calculate the structural stiffness in foot-pounds per degree, weigh the amount of weight (in pounds) placed at the end of the 10-foot bar in order to flex the chassis one degree. Multiply this weight times 10 feet, and this will be the torque.

For example, you applied 523 pounds to the bar. The bar is 10 feet long, so the torque applied is 5,230 foot-pounds. If this is the amount required to flex the chassis one degree, then the structural stiffness of the chassis is 5,230 foot-pounds per degree.

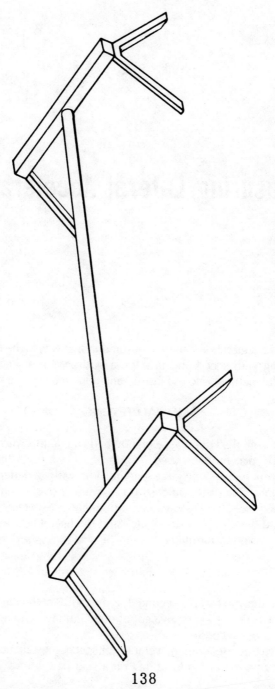

The type of structure we talk about to use in checking the structural stiffness of your chassis.

Measuring Lateral Acceleration

Lateral acceleration can be measured in two ways. The first is by calculating with speed and time on a skid pad. The second, and most useful method, is to use instrumentation on board the race car.

SKID PAD TESTING

To measure the lateral acceleration and calculate it mathematically, a skid pad must be used. A skid pad is simply a flat paved surface, much like any large parking lot, with a perfect circle painted on it. The driver guides his car over the circle as fast as he can possibly hold it in a steady cornering state. The complete circular laps are timed with a stop watch and the lateral acceleration is computed with the formula

$$\frac{v^2}{32(r)}$$

V is the velocity in feet per second. R is the radius of the circle. 32 is a constant which is the equivalent of one G (one G equals 32 feet per second per second).

To solve this equation, the velocity (or speed) must first be calculated. Assume the car is travelling on a skid pad with a 100-foot radius. Then the number of feet the car travels for the complete circle can be figured with the formula for a circumference of a circle:

$$C = 2 \pi r$$

$$C = 2(3.14)(100)$$

$$C = 628$$

If the car travelled that 628 feet in 11.45 seconds, then its velocity in feet per second is 628 feet divided by 11.45 seconds, or 54.84 feet per second.

Now substitute that into the equation for lateral acceleration and solve it:

$$\frac{v^2}{32(r)}$$

$$= \frac{(54.84)^2}{(32(100)}$$

$$= \frac{3007.4}{3200}$$

$$= .94$$

So the lateral acceleration coefficient for this car is .94G.

This means the car's maximum cornering capability is .94 G with the same set of given circumstances which were defined with the car when it was measured. These given circumstances, which can effect the cornering capability of the car, are tires (including size, compound and air pressure), wheel size and offset, tread width, car running height, ballast location, fuel load, springs, antiroll bars, shock absorbers, wheel alignment, total weight and weight distribution. Changing any one of these variables will affect the cornering capability of the car. So, if testing for maximum cornering capability is carried out, the car should be equipped just as it is intended to be used for a particular race track. This type of testing can also be carried out in order to test the effect of each of these variables on the cornering performance of the car. Whatever change results in a higher lateral acceleration is a change which will increase the cornering capability of the car.

140

INSTRUMENTATION

We have developed a mechanical meter called an accelerometer which can be used for testing to measure any type of acceleration in any direction. It measures directly in G's to two decimal points.

The great advantage of this instrument is it can be installed in the car and used on the actual race track. It detects any amount of lateral acceleration at any point, so the car need not be run in just a constant circle.

Another advantage of this instrument is it can be used to determine straightline acceleration and braking G's, to determine optimum shifting points for a car used on a road course, to measure aerodynamic and tire drag, and to act as a dynamometer to measure engine horsepower being delivered at the rear wheels.

A Ford in which we participated in the development and testing. It is shown on a 240-foot diameter skid pad at Mira Loma, California.

Appendix One: Math Fundamentals

Most of us studied algebra, geometry and trigonometry in high school, and that was the end of it. If not practiced daily these mathematical practices can be easily forgotten. We present this chapter for those who have gotten a bit "rusty" in their math skills as some knowledge of math will be required to compute certain formulas in the following chapters.

ALGEBRA FUNDAMENTALS

Algebra is the same as arithmetic only letters are used in algebra to represent the actual numbers. For example:

(1) $$4 \times 2 = 8$$

A similar algebraic statement is:

(2) $$a\,b = c$$

(In algebra, the "x" or multiplication symbol, may be omitted for clarity.) In equation number (2), when the number a is multiplied by the number b, the result (or *product*, as it is properly called) is the number c. If a represents the number 4 and b represents the number 2 then c must represent the number 8. a and b can represent any two numbers whatsoever. But c is always restricted to a particular value which is the product of *a* times *b*.

When we have any algebraic expression such as $a\,b = c$, there are always two other forms of this expression which are always true: If $a\,b = c$, then

(3) $$a = \frac{c}{b}$$

(4) $$b = \frac{c}{a}$$

Equation (3) can be derived by dividing both sides of the equation by the same number, *b*.

$$\frac{ab}{b} = \frac{c}{b}$$

The same number, *b*, divided by the same number, *b*, is always 1. So the equation actually becomes *a* times 1 equals *c* divided by *b*. But the 1 is always omitted from the equation because it has no bearing on the result. Equation (4) is derived in the same manner as explained above.

When an *unknown*, such as *a* in the equation below, is trapped in the middle of an algebraic expression, the equation can be manipulated so that the unknown is isolated on one side of the equal sign so the expression can be easily solved.

$$421 = \frac{8a(9+3)}{115}$$

$$421 = \frac{8a(12)}{115}$$

The first step in simplifying is to perform any operation inside the parenthesis.

$$421(115) = \frac{8a(12)(115)}{115}$$

Multiply both sides of the equation by the bottom number (the denominator) in the division function.

$$421(115) = \frac{8a(12)(115)}{115}$$

The same numbers appearing in the numerator (upper number in a division operation) and denominator cancel each other.

$$48{,}415 = 8a(12)$$

In this step, 48,415 is the result of multiplying 421 times 115.

Both sides of the equation are divided by 12. On the right side the 12 in the denominator cancels the 12 in the numerator.

$$\frac{48,415}{(12)8} = \frac{8a}{8}$$

Both sides of the equation are divided by 8, for the same reason as above. On the left side of the equation, the parenthesis are put around the 12 to indicate it is being multiplied by the 8.

$$\frac{48,415}{96} = a$$

The 96 is the product of multiplying 8 times 12.

$$504.322 = a$$

48,415 has been divided by 96 to give the result (quotient) of 504.322, which is the solution of a.

Many times it is good to substitute the answer you arrived at back into the original equation to be sure that no mistakes were made in the algebraic manipulation.

$$\text{If } 421 = \frac{8a\ (9+3)}{115}$$

$$\text{and } a = 504.322, \text{ then}$$

$$421 = \frac{8(504.322)\ (9+3)}{115}$$

$$421 = \frac{8(504.322)\ (12)}{115}$$

$$421(115) = 8(504.322)12$$

$$48,415 = 4034.576(12)$$

$$48,415 = 48,415$$

MISCELLANEOUS ALGEBRAIC RELATIONSHIPS

Many times in simplifying an algebraic, equation it is helpful to know several useful relationships.

$$\sqrt{\frac{a}{b}} = \frac{\sqrt{a}}{\sqrt{b}}$$

The square root of a fraction equals the square root of the numerator divided by the square root of the denominator.

π

This symbol is the Greek letter *pi*, which is a constant number equal to 3.14.

$a(3+4) = 3a + 4a$

The number on the outside of the parenthesis, *a*, can be multiplied times each function as shown. Usually, this equation is used in reverse for simplification.

$a\left(\dfrac{xy}{b}\right) = \dfrac{a \times y}{b}$

When the number *a* is multiplied by a fraction *a* can be changed into the fraction $\frac{a}{1}$ so that *a* can be combined into the fraction for simplification.

$\dfrac{a}{b} \times \dfrac{x}{y} = \dfrac{ax}{by}$

When fractions are multiplied the numerators are multiplied and the denominators are multiplied.

$\dfrac{c}{d} \div \dfrac{a}{y} = \dfrac{c}{d} \times \dfrac{y}{a}$

To divide by a fraction, invert the numerator and denominator of the fraction you are dividing by and multiply it times the number or fraction to be divided.

$$\dfrac{\frac{a}{b}}{d} = \dfrac{a}{b} \div \dfrac{d}{1} = a \times \dfrac{1}{d} = \dfrac{a}{bd}$$

EXPONENTS

The expression a^n means that the number *a* is multiplied by itself *n* times. The *n* is called the exponent of *a*. For example *a squared* is expressed:

$$a^2 = a \times a$$

a cubed is

$$a^3 = a \times a \times a$$

147

a to the fourth power is

$$a^4 = a \times a \times a \times a$$

The expression $a^n \times a^m$ means that a is multiplied by itself n times and then multiplied by a number which is he product of multiplying a by itself m times. This is the same as multiplying a by itself $n + m$ times. So,

$$a^n \times a^m = a^{n+m}$$

Similarly,

$$\frac{a^n}{a^m} = a^{n-m}$$

GEOMETRY

Although the study of geometry is involved with the relationships of many different shapes, the most important two shapes for us to consider here is the right triangle and the circle.

CIRCLES

The illustrations below depict the various concepts associated with a circle. They should be self explanatory.

We might add as a bit of advice here that in working with formulas involving the radius and diameter of a circle the two terms are many times confused. Be sure that you are using the correct, value either radius or diameter, when working with formulas.

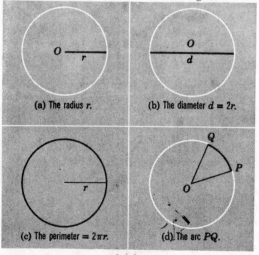

(a) The radius r.

(b) The diameter $d = 2r$.

(c) The perimeter $= 2\pi r$.

(d) The arc PQ.

THE RIGHT TRIANGLE

This triangle is so named because it always has one of its angles equal to 90 degrees. Because the sum of all three angles of any triangle equal 180 degrees, the other two angles of the right triangle must add up to 90 degrees.

All right triangles have a side called the *hypotenuse*. This side is always the one opposite the 90° angle.

Right triangles always conform to Pythagoras' theorem which states: "The square of the hypotenuse length is equal to the sum of the squares of the other two side lengths." For the right triangle we have illustrated here, $a^2 + b^2 = c^2$. If $a = 3$ and $b = 4$, then:

$$3^2 + 4^2 = c^2$$
$$9 + 16 = c^2$$
$$25 = c^2$$
$$\sqrt{25} = \sqrt{c^2}$$
$$5 = c$$

The relationship of $a^2 + b^2 = c^2$ is employed in many forms to help find the missing dimensions of a triangle.

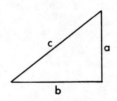

TRIGONOMETRY

In our review of basic trigonometry here, we are concerned with the three major trigonomic functions, sine, cosine and tangent.

In any right triangle when one angle is specified, there is a side of the triangle which is adjacent to the angle. Also, there is a side which is opposite from the angle. And last, there is always the hypotenuse side.

Sine, cosine and tangent are simply the ratio relationships of one side to another. The illustrations and definitions below should explain these ratios clearly.

149

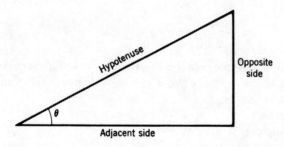

Figure 1   The right triangle used to define the trigonometric functions.

$$\sin \theta = \frac{\text{Length of opposite side}}{\text{Length of hypotenuse}}$$

$$\cos \theta = \frac{\text{Length of adjacent side}}{\text{Length of hypotenuse}}$$

$$\tan \theta = \frac{\text{Length of opposite side}}{\text{Length of adjacent side}}$$

To understand how these trigonomic relationships are used, let's look at some examples. In the triangle below, we know the lengths of two sides and we want to know what the angle is that is marked. The opposite side (5) is known and the adjacent side (3) is known. Therefore we find a formula which has both of these in it:

$$\tan \theta = \frac{\text{opp}}{\text{adj}}$$

$$\tan \theta = \frac{5}{3}$$

$$\tan \theta = 1.666$$

Once we have solved the problem this far, we consult a trig table to find the value of tan = 1.666. We find it is 59 degrees. (For your convenience, there is a trig table which follows this chapter.)

Another example:

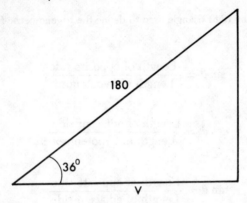

What is the length of v?

$$\cos \theta = \frac{adj}{hyp}$$

$$\cos 36° = \frac{v}{180}$$

(From the trig table we find the cosine of 36° is .809.)

$$.809 = \frac{v}{180}$$

$$.809(180) = v$$

$$145.62 = v$$

Note: There are 60 minutes in one degree. If an angle is expressed in degrees and minutes, it is much easier to work with it expressed in a decimal. For example, 9°29' equals $9\frac{29}{60}$ or 9.48 degrees.

VECTORS

A vector is used to determine a magnitude or direction in a plane which is not perfectly horizontal or vertical. Vectors are solved through the use of trigonometry.

The length of the vector is directly proportional to the magnitude of the quantity in question, such as force, velocity or acceleration.

To understand how a vector is resolved into its two component parts, it is best to study an example. As shown in the accompanying drawing, a car is travelling northeast at 50 miles per hour. How fast is it travelling east?

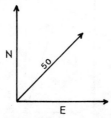

The term of northeast implies the amount of travel in the east direction is the same as the amount of travel in the north direction. When north and east are laid out on a scale, their intersection forms a 90-degree angle, and since the northeast travel, or vector, equally intersects that angle, we have a known angle of 45 degrees.

The other known we have is the magnitude of the northeast vector, 50 miles per hour. So now we can use the trigonometric equation

$$\text{Cos} = \frac{adj}{hyp}$$

In this case, the hypotenuse is 50° and the angle is 45°, so we are seeking the length of the adjacent. In the trig table, we find the value of "cosine 45" to be .707, so the equation to solve for the adjacent side is:

$$.707 = \frac{adj}{50}$$

$$50(.707) = adj$$

$$35.35 = adj$$

So, the car is travelling 35.35 miles per hour in the east direction.

Another example: a equals 2,830 and b equals 205. What is the magnitude of the resultant vector (r)?

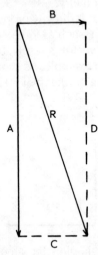

To start we have only one known quantity on each side of a triangle (a and b), with hypotenuse unknown. It is impossible to know the angles, unless the problem is drawn out to scale. So, a rectangle is drawn with dotted lines. Side c is equal to side b and side d is equal to side a. Now two sides are known. To solve for the vector, we use the Pythagorean theorum:

$$(opp)^2 + (adj)^2 = (hyp)^2$$

$$(2,830)^2 + (205)^2 = (hyp)^2$$

$$8,008,900 + 42,025 = (hyp)^2$$

$$8,050,925 = (hyp)^2$$

$$\sqrt{8,050,925} = hyp$$

$$2,837.4 = hyp$$

Appendix Two: Trig Tables

Angle	Sin	Cos	Tan
0	0	1.0	0
.5	.008	.999	.008
.6	.01	.999	.010
.8	.013	.999	.013
1.0	.017	.999	.017
1.2	.02	.999	.020
1.4	.024	.999	.024
1.6	.027	.999	.027
1.8	.031	.999	.031
2.0	.035	.999	.035
2.2	.038	.999	.038
2.4	.042	.999	.042
2.6	.045	.998	.045
2.8	.049	.998	.049
3.0	.052	.998	.052
3.2	.056	.998	.056
3.4	.059	.998	.059
3.6	.063	.998	.063
3.8	.066	.997	.066
4.0	.07	.997	.070
4.2	.073	.997	.073
4.4	.077	.997	.077
4.6	.080	.996	.080
4.8	.083	.996	.083

Angle	Sin	Cos	Tan
5.0	.087	.996	.088
5.5	.096	.995	.098
6.0	.104	.994	.105
6.5	.113	.994	.114
7.0	.122	.992	.123
7.5	.130	.991	.132
8.0	.139	.990	.140
8.5	.148	.989	.150
9.0	.156	.988	.158
9.5	.165	.986	.167
10.0	.174	.985	.176
10.5	.182	.983	.185
11.0	.191	.982	.194
11.5	.199	.980	.204
12.0	.208	.978	.213
12.5	.216	.976	.222
13.0	.225	.974	.231
13.5	.233	.972	.240
14.0	.242	.970	.249
14.5	.250	.968	.259
15.0	.259	.966	.268
15.5	.267	.964	.277
16.0	.276	.961	.287
16.5	.284	.959	.296
17.0	.292	.956	.306
17.5	.301	.954	.315
18.0	.309	.951	.325
18.5	.317	.948	.335
19.0	.326	.946	.344
19.5	.334	.943	.354
20.0	.342	.940	.364
20.5	.350	.937	.374
21	.358	.934	.384
21.5	.366	.930	.394
22	.375	.927	.404
22.5	.383	.924	.414
23	.391	.920	.424
23.5	.399	.917	.435
24	.407	.914	.445
24.5	.415	.910	.456
25	.423	.906	.466
25.5	.430	.903	.477

Angle	Sin	Cos	Tan
26	.438	.899	.488
26.5	.446	.895	.499
27	.454	.891	.510
27.5	.462	.887	.521
28	.470	.883	.532
28.5	.477	.879	.543
29	.485	.875	.554
29.5	.492	.870	.566
30	.500	.866	.577
30.5	.508	.862	.589
31	.515	.857	.601
31.5	.522	.853	.613
32	.530	.848	.625
32.5	.537	.843	.637
33	.545	.839	.649
33.5	.552	.834	.662
34	.559	.829	.674
34.5	.566	.824	.687
35	.574	.819	.700
35.5	.581	.814	.713
36	.588	.809	.726
36.5	.595	.804	.740
37	.602	.799	.754
37.5	.609	.793	.767
38	.616	.788	.781
38.5	.622	.783	.795
39	.629	.777	.810
39.5	.636	.772	.824
40	.643	.766	.839
40.5	.649	.760	.854
41	.656	.755	.869
41.5	.663	.749	.885
42	.669	.743	.900
42.5	.676	.737	.916
43	.682	.731	.932
43.5	.688	.725	.949
44	.695	.719	.966
44.5	.701	.713	.983
45	.707	.707	1.0

Appendix Three

GLOSSARY OF HANDLING AND SUSPENSION TERMS

Acceleration .... The rate at which the speed of an object changes over a specified period of time. The acceleration of one gravity (one G) is a change of 32 feet per second over a period of one second.

Arm (lever) .... A rigid bar or beam capable of turning about one point called a fulcrum. An arm is used to transfer rotating motion into lateral movement or vice versa.

Bending .... The load on a structural component causing it to curve.

Bump .... The upward movement of a suspension component from its static position. Also called jounce or compression.

Camber .... The inward or outward tilt of the wheel at the top.

Caster .... The backward or forward tilt of the steering axis pivot point.

Center of gravity .... An imaginary point about which the vehicle's weight is balanced.

Compliance .... The compression of a flexible suspension component under loading. For example, a soft rubber bushing which compresses under cornering load (an undesirable condition in a racing vehicle).

Curb weight .... The net weight of a vehicle including a full supply of fuel, oil and water, but no passengers.

Distortion .... A twisting or twisted condition.

Dynamic .... Opposite of static.

Frequency .... The number of vibrations, oscillations, cycles or changes in direction in a unit of time.

Hotchkiss drive .... The conventional solid rear axle drive system found under the rear of most American passenger cars.

Kingpin inclination ...... Same as steering axis inclination.

Leverage .... The mechanical advantage gained by the use of a lever.

Load .... The force applied to a structural member.

MacPherson system ..... A suspension system which incorporates a coil spring-over-shock unit together in an upright strut to serve as a locating member for a spindle.

Period .... The time interval at which maximum vibration occurs.

Pitch .... The rear-to-front (and reverse) rocking motion of a vehicle.

Radius .... The distance from a center of a circle to the circumference, or from the center of rotation to the arc.

Rebound .... Opposite of bump.

Roll .... The circular motion of a vehicle body rotating about its centerline axis away from the direction of turn it makes.

Shim .... A spacer to adjust a distance between two parts.

Slip angle .... The angle between the true centerline of the tire and the actual tire path when in a turn.

Shock absorber .... A hydraulic device used to dampen or stabilize the up and down motion of the car's chassis by controlling the compression and rebound movement of the springs.

Static .... The conditions of the car at rest—not in motion.

Stiffness .... The complete resistance to any deflecting.

Stress .... A load or force applied to a defined area. Its most common expression is in pounds per square inch.

Tire contact patch ...... The pattern made by the tire in its contact with the road surface.

Toe-out, toe-in ....The difference in distance between the front tires at the extreme front and extreme rear at spindle height, when the wheels are in the straight ahead position.

Torque ....A force that tends to produce a rotating or turning motion.

Torsion ....twist

Track ....Same as tread width.

Transient ....Unpredictable change or effect.

Tread width ....The distance between the vertical centerlines of the tires on an axle.

Upsprung weight ....The weight of that part of a vehicle which is not supported by the springs.

Powers and Roots

n	n^2	n^3	$\sqrt{n}$	$\sqrt[3]{n}$
1	1	1	1.0000000	1.0000000
2	4	8	1.4142136	1.2599210
3	9	27	1.7320508	1.4422496
4	16	64	2.0000000	1.5874011
5	25	125	2.2360680	1.7099759
6	36	216	2.4494897	1.8171206
7	49	343	2.6457513	1.9129312
8	64	512	2.8284271	2.0000000
9	81	729	3.0000000	2.0800838
10	100	1000	3.1622777	2.1544347
11	121	1331	3.3166248	2.2239801
12	144	1728	3.4641016	2.2894285
13	169	2197	3.6055513	2.3513347
14	196	2744	3.7416574	2.4101423
15	225	3375	3.8729833	2.4662121
16	256	4096	4.0000000	2.5198421
17	289	4913	4.1231056	2.5712816
18	324	5832	4.2426407	2.6207414
19	361	6859	4.3588989	2.6684016
20	400	8000	4.4721360	2.7144176
21	441	9261	4.5825757	2.7589242
22	484	10648	4.6904158	2.8020393
23	529	12167	4.7958315	2.8438670
24	576	13824	4.8989795	2.8844991
25	625	15625	5.0000000	2.9240177
26	676	17576	5.0990195	2.9624961
27	729	19683	5.1961524	3.0000000
28	784	21952	5.2915026	3.0365890
29	841	24389	5.3851648	3.0723168
30	900	27000	5.4772256	3.1072325
31	961	29791	5.5677644	3.1413807
32	1024	32768	5.6568542	3.1748021
33	1089	35937	5.7445626	3.2075343
34	1156	39304	5.8309519	3.2396118
35	1225	42875	5.9160798	3.2710663

Powers and Roots (Continued)

n	n^2	n^3	$\sqrt{n}$	$\sqrt[3]{n}$
36	1296	46656	6.0000000	3.3019272
37	1369	50653	6.0827625	3.3322219
38	1444	54872	6.1644140	3.3619754
39	1521	59319	6.2449980	3.3912114
40	1600	64000	6.3245553	3.4199519
41	1681	68921	6.4031242	3.4482172
42	1764	74088	6.4807407	3.4760266
43	1849	79507	6.5574385	3.5033981
44	1936	85184	6.6332496	3.5303483
45	2025	91125	6.7082039	3.5568933
46	2116	97336	6.7823300	3.5830479
47	2209	103823	6.8556546	3.6088261
48	2304	110592	6.9282032	3.6342412
49	2401	117649	7.0000000	3.6593057
50	2500	125000	7.0710678	3.6840315
51	2601	132651	7.1414284	3.7084298
52	2704	140608	7.2111026	3.7325112
53	2809	148877	7.2801099	3.7562858
54	2916	157464	7.3484692	3.7797631
55	3025	166375	7.4161985	3.8029525
56	3136	175616	7.4833148	3.8258624
57	3249	185193	7.5498344	3.8485011
58	3364	195112	7.6157731	3.8708766
59	3481	205379	7.6811457	3.8929964
60	3600	216000	7.7459667	3.9148676
61	3721	226981	7.8102497	3.9364972
62	3844	238328	7.8740079	3.9578916
63	3969	250047	7.9372539	3.9790572
64	4096	262144	8.0000000	4.0000000
65	4225	274625	8.0622577	4.0207258
66	4356	287496	8.1240384	4.0412400
67	4489	300763	8.1853528	4.0615481
68	4624	314432	8.2462113	4.0816551
69	4761	328509	8.3066239	4.1015659
70	4900	343000	8.3666003	4.1212853

Powers and Roots (Continued)

n	n²	n³	√n	³√n
71	5041	357911	8.4261498	4.1408177
72	5184	373248	8.4852814	4.1601676
73	5329	389017	8.5440037	4.1793392
74	5476	405224	8.6023253	4.1983365
75	5625	421875	8.6602540	4.2171633
76	5776	438976	8.7177979	4.2358236
77	5929	456533	8.7749644	4.2543209
78	6084	474552	8.8317609	4.2726587
79	6241	493039	8.8881944	4.2908404
80	6400	512000	8.9442719	4.3088694
81	6561	531441	9.0000000	4.3267487
82	6724	551368	9.0553851	4.3444815
83	6889	571787	9.1104336	4.3620707
84	7056	592704	9.1651514	4.3795191
85	7225	614125	9.2195445	4.3968297
86	7396	636056	9.2736185	4.4140050
87	7569	658503	9.3273791	4.4310476
88	7744	681472	9.3808315	4.4479602
89	7921	704969	9.4339811	4.4647451
90	8100	729000	9.4868330	4.4814047
91	8281	753571	9.5393920	4.4979414
92	8464	778688	9.5916630	4.5143574
93	8649	804357	9.6436508	4.5306549
94	8836	830584	9.6953597	4.5468359
95	9025	857375	9.7467943	4.5629026
96	9216	884736	9.7979590	4.5788570
97	9409	912673	9.8488578	4.5947009
98	9604	941192	9.8994949	4.6104363
99	9801	970299	9.9498744	4.6260650
100	10000	1000000	10.0000000	4.6415888

DECIMAL EQUIVALENTS

Fraction of Inch	Decimal of Inch	Decimal Millimeters	Fraction of Inch	Decimal of Inch	Decimal Millimeters
1/64....	.015625	0.39688	33/64...	.515625	13.09690
1/32.....	.03125	0.79375	17/32......	.53125	13.49378
3/64....	.046875	1.19063	35/64...	.546875	13.89065
1/16..........	.0625	1.58750	9/16..........	.5625	14.28753
5/64....	.078125	1.98438	37/64...	.578125	14.68440
3/32.......	.09375	2.38125	19/32.....	.59375	15.08128
7/64....	.109375	2.77813	39/64...	.609375	15.47816
1/8..........	.125	3.17501	5/8..........	.625	15.87503
9/64....	.140625	3.57188	41/64...	.640625	16.27191
5/32.......	.15625	3.96876	21/32.....	.65625	16.66878
11/64....	.171875	4.36563	43/64...	.671875	17.06566
3/16...	.1875	4.76251	11/16..........	.6875	17.46253
13/64...	.203125	5.15939	45/64...	.703125	17.85941
7/32.......	.21875	5.55626	23/32.....	.71875	18.25629
15/64...	.234375	5.95314	47/64...	.734375	18.65316
1/4..........	.25	6.35001	3/4..........	.75	19.05004
17/64...	.265625	6.74689	49/64...	.765625	19.44691
9/32.....	.28125	7.14376	25/32.....	.78125	19.84379
19/64...	.296875	7.54064	51/64...	.796875	20.24067
5/16..........	.3125	7.93752	13/16..........	.8125	20.63754
21/64...	.328125	8.33439	53/64...	.828125	21.03442
11/32......	.34375	8.73127	27/32.....	.84375	21.43129
23/64...	.359375	9.12814	55/64...	.859375	21.82817
3/8..........	.375	9.52502	7/8..........	.875	22.22504
25/64...	.390625	9.92189	57/64...	.890625	22.62192
13/32......	.40625	10.31877	29/32.....	.90625	23.01880
27/64...	.421875	10.71565	59/64...	.921875	23.41567
7/16..........	.4375	11.11252	15/16..........	.9375	23.81255
29/64...	.453125	11.50940	61/64...	.953125	24.20942
15/32......	.46875	11.90627	31/32.....	.96875	24.60630
31/64...	.484375	12.30315	63/64...	.984375	25.00318
1/2..........	.5	12.70003	1..............	1.	25.40005

Speed Conversion Factors

$$FPS \times .6818 = MPH$$
$$MPH \times 1.467 = FPS$$

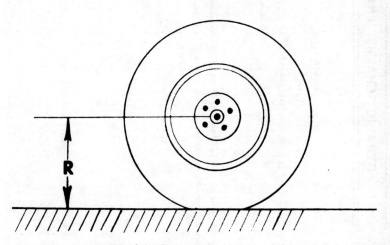

"R" is the rolling radius of the tire.

DYNAMIC CHASSIS ANALYSIS

Specifications

1. Weight (total) _____

2. Weight Distribution: LF _____ RF _____
   LR _____ RR _____

3. Weight (sprung): LF _____ RF _____
   LR _____ RR _____

4. Tread width: Front _____
   Rear _____
   Average _____

5. Spring rates: LF _____ RF _____
   LR _____ RR _____

6. Motion ratio squared: F _____ R _____

7. Wheel rates: LF _____ RF _____
   LR _____ RR _____

8. CGH _____

9. Roll axis to CGH _____

10. Wheelbase _____

Analysis

1. Total effective wheel rate force
   LF _____
   RF _____
   LR _____
   RR _____
   Bar _____
   +
   Total _____

2. Roll couple distribution
   (front wheel rate force divided by total
   wheel rate force)
   % front roll couple _____

3. Weight transferred during cornering _____

4. Dynamic total weight distribution:
   LF _____ RF _____
   LR _____ RR _____

5. Overturning moment _____

6. Total roll stiffness _____

7. Total chassis roll (in degrees) _____

8. Outside wheel travel ($M_{ot} - M_r = 0$) _____

9. Suspension frequencies:
   RF _____
   RR _____

DYNAMIC CHASSIS ANALYSIS

Specifications

1. Weight (total) _____

2. Weight Distribution: LF _____ RF _____
                         LR _____ RR _____

3. Weight (sprung):   LF _____ RF _____
                         LR _____ RR _____

4. Tread width: Front _____
                 Rear _____
                 Average _____

5. Spring rates: LF _____ RF _____
                         LR _____ RR _____

6. Motion ratio squared: F _____ R _____

7. Wheel rates: LF _____ RF _____
                         LR _____ RR _____

8. CGH _____

9. Roll axis to CGH _____

10. Wheelbase _____

Analysis

1. Total effective wheel rate force

   LF _____

   RF _____

   LR _____

   RR _____

   Bar _____

   + _____

   Total _____

2. Roll couple distribution
   (front wheel rate force divided by total
   wheel rate force)

   % front roll couple _____

3. Weight transferred during cornering _____

4. Dynamic total weight distribution:

   LF _____ RF _____

   LR _____ RR _____

5. Overturning moment _____

6. Total roll stiffness _____

7. Total chassis roll (in degrees) _____

8. Outside wheel travel ($M_{ot} - M_r = 0$) _____

9. Suspension frequencies:

   RF _____

   RR _____

DYNAMIC CHASSIS ANALYSIS

Specifications

1. Weight (total) _____

2. Weight Distribution: LF _____ RF _____
                        LR _____ RR _____

3. Weight (sprung): LF _____ RF _____
                     LR _____ RR _____

4. Tread width: Front _____
                Rear _____
                Average _____

5. Spring rates: LF _____ RF _____
                  LR _____ RR _____

6. Motion ratio squared: F _____ R _____

7. Wheel rates: LF _____ RF _____
                 LR _____ RR _____

8. CGH _____

9. Roll axis to CGH _____

10. Wheelbase _____

Analysis

1. Total effective wheel rate force

   LF _____
   RF _____
   LR _____
   RR _____
   Bar _____
   + _____
   Total _____

2. Roll couple distribution

   (front wheel rate force divided by total
   wheel rate force)

   % front roll couple _____

3. Weight transferred during cornering _____

4. Dynamic total weight distribution:

   LF _____ RF _____
   LR _____ RR _____

5. Overturning moment _____

6. Total roll stiffness _____

7. Total chassis roll (in degrees) _____

8. Outside wheel travel ($M_{ot} - M_r = 0$) _____

9. Suspension frequencies:

   RF _____
   RR _____

Work Book For Advanced Race Car Suspension Development

Order #WB5...$4.95

We publish a Work Book for Advanced Race Car Suspension Development which is designed to accompany this book. We strongly urge that you purchase it to aid in your understanding of the material in this book, as well as gaining a better understanding of your particular car.

Other books from Steve Smith Autosports

Building The Hobby Stock/Street Stock Car

This book is written for the low-buck racer with limited facilities and who wants to farm out a minimum of work. It shows you how to build a car with a minimum of "store-bought" parts or expensive machine work. Chapters include: your choice of car • cage construction • chassis vs. unitized car • engine, cooling and electrics • transmissions and rear ends • tires and wheels • suspension (parts choice, building and sorting) • driving • spare parts and preparation. **Order** #S126...$7.95

The Stock Car Racing Chassis

This is a basic handling and suspension book with facts on caster, camber, toe-out, tire temperatures and sorting a chassis. Special feature is the well-illustrated chapter on building a competitive Chevelle chassis. Order #S101...$6.00

The Complete Stock Car Chassis Guide

A handling and suspension book discussing racing tire principles and selection, dirt track chassis design, roll cage construction, shock absorber selection, how to build the two-point suspension, aerodynamics, roll couple, anti-roll bars and much more. Packed with photos and drawings. **Order** #S102...$6.00

Coil-Over Suspension Design Booklet

An 8-page booklet packed with drawings and photos showing the methods and theories behind using the coil-over suspension system, mounting techniques and proper cage and chassis construction. Order #BC201...$5.95

Other books from Steve Smith Autosports

Dirt Track Chassis Technology

A dynamite source book for the changing, and most innovative form of racing. A nuts-and-bolts discussion of every facet of dirt track racing, including: specific chassis set-up recommendations • how to judge and adjust for changing track • side bite • leaf springs vs. coil springs • proper weight distrib. • details of the new 5-spring coil/over suspension • tires • shock absorbers • front and rear suspension systems • chassis construction • aerodynamics • preparation tips, plus much, much more. Packed with helpful photos and diagrams, plus the best state-of-the-art racing information. For the veteran or novice, a book you shouldn't be without. **Order #S133...** **$9.95**

Engine Builder's Notebook

An 8-page booklet you can use to store all your info and specs for each engine you build. Lists every engine building step in correct order. A real frustration saver. **Order #S121 ...$3.95**

Race Car Fabrication And Preparation

Includes thorough discussions of: prepping a transmission • setting up the rear end • electrical system • building the chassis and roll cage • cutting costs and beating the economy stock rules • welding • clutches • safety systems • wrecking yard parts • fabrication • hardware • wheels and tires • cooling system • plumbing • driveshafts • Plus much, much more. Photo packed, over 160 pages. **Order #S114...$8.95**

Racing The Small Block Chevy

An all new book rewritten in Fall, 1979, to bring you completely up to date. Everything you need to get the most power from your engine. Contents: The very latest inside information • tested and proven facts from NASCAR engine builders and Smokey Yunick • revealing info on cams, carburetor mods, head porting • the entire engine & assembly discussed in detail. **Order #S112...$7.95**

The Racer's Complete Reference Guide

This book is the "Yellow Pages" of the high performance world. Tells you who makes it and where to find it for parts, hardware, services, anything. Says Stock Car Racing Magazine "The book is a handy guide to the makers and suppliers of parts and services. This book's a bible you can't be without!" All new 4th edition released December, 1980. **Order #S108...$6.95**

Racing Engine Preparation

A.J. Foyt says, "This is the most complete engine book I've ever seen. No nonsense...very thorough." Uses the small block Chevy, Ford and MoPar as examples. Chapters include: understanding camshafts • lubrication system • ignition • complete listing of major part numbers • detailed engine assembly • cylinder head blueprinting • dyno testing. Plus preparation of rods, pistons, carburetors, blocks and much more. 152 pages, 380 photos. **Order #S106...$8.95**

Published by

STEVE SMITH
AUTOSPORTS
PUBLICATIONS

P.O. Box 11631/Santa Ana, CA 92711/(714) 639-7681